GEORGIST PARADI(
Series Editor: Fred Harrison ʀɴᴏᴄ

A Philosophy
for a Fair Society

Michael Hudson, G.J. Miller & Kris Feder

The Georgist Paradigm is a model of political economy
that offers comprehensive solutions to the social and
ecological problems of our age. At its heart are principles
on land rights and public finance which integrate economic
efficiency with social justice.

Shepheard-Walwyn (Publishers) Ltd.

in association with

Centre for Incentive Taxation Ltd.

First published in 1994 by
Shepheard-Walwyn (Publishers) Ltd.,
26 Charing Cross Road (Suite 34),
London WC2H ODH

in association with

Centre for Incentive Taxation Ltd.,
177 Vauxhall Bridge Road,
London SW1V 1EU.
Tel: 071 834 4266 Fax: 071 834 4979

British Library Cataloguing in Publication Data

A catalogue record of this book
is available from the British Library

Hdbk ISBN 0 85683 161 1
Ppbk ISBN 0 85683 159 X

Printed and bound in Great Britain by
BPC Wheatons, Exeter.

Contents

Prologue
The Archaeology of Economic Collapse:
A 4000 Year Perspective

Michael Hudson and Fred Harrison

W HAT is wrong with today's economy? WHEN and WHY did things start to go wrong? And HOW can we restore social and environmental harmony for the third millennium?

Despite the explosion in scholarship and political activism during the 20th century, we still do not have coherent answers to these questions. More books have been published in the past generation than in all of preceding history, yet like commercial television their subject matter has narrowed to absorb our attention without engaging our minds with respect to the great problem of our age: how to (re)structure our society and the world economy in which we live. If this is the Information Age, it threatens to bury the search for truth and insight under a crust of trivial distraction.

More people are graduating from universities than ever before, yet the social-science curriculum has narrowed to produce what Thorstein Veblen called an "educated incapacity" to recognize the flaws implanted in our economy, highlighted by the trained incompetence of professional economists.

Will society rise to the challenge? Unless we produce new diagnoses and practical solutions, the 21st century may prove to be a re-run of the past 100 years: more global poverty, ecological strangulation and commercialization of culture.

These are the time-honoured criteria of decadence. Indeed, future historians may gaze back in amazement on how narrowly the minds of

7

economic and political managers have focused on the short term and on the bottom line of the balance sheet even as society careered over the precipice.

Yet there is a bright side to the corner into which the economy has painted itself. If today's world stands at a philosophical crossroads, such crises are accompanied by a renewed spirit of enquiry. These windows of intellectual opportunity are rare, for society normally is closed around a body of beliefs and rules that form the basis for going about its daily business. It takes periods of social breakdown to provide social and ideological flexibility.

The first such expressions usually have difficulty rising above the trivial, to be sure. Anti-heroes precede heroes, and their first characteristic is a cynicism towards authority. Normally law-abiding people opt out of the mainstream by flouting laws and social conventions, pursuing self-centered lifestyles which offer the semblance of a new identity but which lack the politically binding force needed to consolidate new social takeoffs. The virtual reality of new electronic headsets is not yet a new social reality.

All we can say at present is that the ground is being prepared by wiping the intellectual slate clean of the paradigms that have guided private action and public policy during the industrial era. As these policies fall into disrepute, they create a culture fertile for the growth of new alternatives.

In the wake of Stalinism's death, socialism has not moved to reassert itself. Academic Marxism has moved more toward becoming a theory of language, of literary and ideological deconstruction rather than analyzing the quandaries of modern *rentier* capitalism. Yet even as socialism has been eclipsed in the former Soviet sphere, few countries in the West are convinced that our own particular brand of finance-capitalism has the binding force that is an essential ingredient of a sustainable social system. If the spectre of capitalist economic bubbles is haunting the new Russia (with the collapse of the MMM stock-market Ponzi scheme wiping out the savings of five to ten million Russian investors), the spectre of *rentier* parasitism and its debt-burdened insolvency are haunting the rest of the world economy.

The great irony is that capitalism's victory over communism seems to be coinciding with capitalism itself succumbing to a *rentier* cancer – one which the economics profession is welcoming breathlessly as "postindustrialism" rather than calling it obsolescence.

If the economy is becoming obsolescent, then so is its guiding body of theory. This is the basic truth that most economists are professionally unable to acknowledge.

The authors of this volume offer an antidote, a framework to interpret the past, present and future in terms of a paradigm that neo-classical economics has vulgarized and misrepresented to the point where policy-makers have found it easy to ignore.

The *when* and *why* questions are confonted in the first study. In a series of waves of privatization extending over some four thousand years, our civilization has dropped its once-traditional ideology of periodic economic renewal in favour of irreversible linear progress. Under the circumstances, this means aggravating existing inequality and moving yet deeper into our quandary rather than acting to renew economic balance and cohesion. The result is that our particular brand of progress has been accompanied by a spreading poverty, burdened by debt accruals and the unaccounted cleanup costs (both social and ecological) that are needed to undo what economic self-centredness has left out of its balance sheets and bottom lines.

Dr. Miller, a clinical scientist, confronts the *what* question. Despite the humanitarianism that has guided social evolution during the past century of welfare capitalism, not every able-bodied person is enabled to earn a decent living by the sweat of his or her brow. The Welfare State was supposed to reduce disparities of income and wealth through the progressive taxation of higher incomes. It promised to create conditions for decent living for those who, by age or ailment, were not able to provide for themselves. Instead, the life chances of those at the bottom of society are either no better, or are even worse today than a century ago. The concentration of wealth into fewer hands continues apace even to the point where it is now the rich, not the needy, that receive most economic welfare from society at large.

The Welfare State – capitalism without risk, at least for the richest and most powerful – has become a social system to which we need to attach a Health Hazard warning. But what is the alternative? How can we devise a social system able to evolve sympathetically from current institutions so that the changeover need not involve a brutal "shock therapy"? This is the question addressed by Dr. Feder, an economics professor who reviews the problem of *how* to liberate people by providing them with the economic freedom to pursue the good life.

The privatization syndrome

Analysis of contemporary problems requires a cultural context. In our view, we need an appreciation of the sources of the friction points in our social system. These are traced back to what we call the privatization process. Economic polarization, financial strangulation and tax avoidance by the wealthiest property owners have been distinctive features of societies ever since Sumer yielded to Akkadian and Babylonian conquest over four thousand years ago. At first these problems were overcome, but matters reached an unprecedented critical mass with the Roman oligarchy's law of property, the land seizures of the Norman invasions and fiscal overlordship of Europe, and the modern financial indebtedness of the land and indeed, entire nations.

What would strike any visitor from antiquity as most remarkable would be our economic ideology. No Stoic or other philosopher proposed that Rome avert economic stagnation by sponsoring industrial corporations to borrow Roman savings and invest them productively. Debt was viewed as the surest path to perdition, in an epoch where productive borrowing was unknown. No philosophers advocated a self-expanding consumer-driven society. Just the opposite: they wanted to withdraw into austerity, idealizing the past and its image of the Noble Savage. The Bronze Age appeared to classical philosophers as having been a Golden Age, one that subsequently was corrupted by self-centredness, appropriation of the land and the consequent falling of entire economies into debt.

What shines through Livy's *History of Rome*, Plutarch's *Parallel Lives of the Famous Greeks and Romans*, Solon's poetry and his political acts is a decrying of the dynamics of usurious debt burdening grinding society to a halt, and the addictive *hubris* of wealth expressed most notoriously in monopolization of the land and money. This economic *hubris* forms the subject of the best early Greek poetry, such as that of Theognis and Archilochus.

Yet land privatization, debt, and the need to shape public laws and market relations so as to harmonise the private pursuit of wealth with the public interest are the most conspicuous blind spots in neo-classical economics. As an academic discipline, this narrow-minded economics was sponsored a century ago to replace classical political economy. It was the product of a well-financed campaign by men who had grown rich by monopolizing land, minerals, oil and other natural, once-public resources, and by financial manipulations and stock watering.

These twin *rentier* interests – rent-takers and interest-takers – joined hands to create a new orthodoxy. One fount of economic shortsightedness was the University of Chicago, the legacy of John D. Rockefeller's Standard Oil fortune. Another early fount was Columbia University, expressing the economic philosophy most congenial to J. P. Morgan's Wall Street managers. From such academic nodes the new teachings came to pass for economic objectivity by an equally well-financed Congress and network of "public-interest" institutions.

The seeds of civilization's long evolution along the privatization path – indeed, the path to debt-financed privatization – may be found even earlier, in the collapse of Bronze Age Mesopotamian society at the end of the third millennium BC. This experience, history's first Dark Age, shows how the *privatization syndrome* initially resulted from military overlayerings of one people (in this case, the Sumerians) by alien conquerors who parcelled out the land among their own ranks, and then supplemented the rent-lever with the debt lever to extract the economic surplus.

As in medieval England, the Mesopotamian overlayering blocked society's ability to serve the interests of its component local groups. The economic surplus, hitherto used to maintain the local community's infrastructure – including export handicraft production in Sumer's case – was diverted to pay tribute to alien appropriators. Assets were stripped rather than productively managed. This asset stripping went hand in hand with deepening poverty for most people, ending in ecological and military disaster, even before there was a World Bank and IMF to give their economic blessing to the looting of man and nature by saying that all this made perfect economic sense as an "austerity program."

Modern scholarship provides a chronological sequence of developments in antiquity which, to use a biological analogy, were rogue genes spliced onto the cultural DNA of Western civilization:

• **territorial conquest**, leading imperial conquerors to rely on local client chieftains for support, relinquishing more and more local authority to them, enabling them to engage in local exploitation, personal appropriation of the land, and consequent rack-renting.

• **monopolization of the soil** at the expense of social self-support and

fiscal collections, ultimately strangling the central government apparatus.
   • **unproductive interest-bearing debt** kept on the books rather than being cancelled when it grows to overburden society's debt-paying capacity.
   • **failure periodically to restore economic order**, letting creditors monopolize the land and other hitherto public resources *irreversibly*.

Territorial conquest The earliest conquerors of agricultural societies were obliged to preserve the primordial right of access to the land. At first the victors demanded what they could get in the form of whatever payment of movable wealth could be extracted on the spot – precious metals, slave women and other time-honoured trophies of war. In time, however, the land itself was made to yield its usufruct to foreign conquerors.[1]

   The land ethic of these conquerors, from Sargon's Akkadians to those of imperial Rome and, later, the medieval Normans and other Viking invaders, had the effect of undermining the customary social balance. As the combination of foreign tribute and the spread of local warfare throughout the archaic world elevated war chiefs to commanding positions, territorial conquest became an instrument for the ruler's own personal aggrandizement. The economic consequence of war no longer was merely a transfer of surplus movable wealth, but an ongoing support for oppressive regimes.

   The result was an organization of warfare on unprecedented terms. Local headmen and imperial bureaucrats came to equate power with depriving local populations of their land-rights. This expropriation of the land was backed by the development of usurious credit. Interest was calculated on the arrears that resulted when local populations were unable to pay the tribute or other public fees that were levied. By Roman times, empires tried to seize from abroad the economic surplus they no longer could produce at home, as a result of their drying up the domestic market and reducing freemen and their families to economic bondage.

Forfeiture of land-tenure rights The archaic natural order had vested every community member with personal rights of access to the land as the basic means of self-support. These customary rights defined a family's freedom to live independently rather than for others.

   However, there were times and circumstances when wars called men away from their land to fight. Some were wounded or even killed, or captured and held for ransom. Floods, droughts or insect infestations might ravage the land. In such circumstances cultivators had to pledge their land-rights to creditors. This was to become a defining characteristic of civilization – a progressive alienation of people from the land, initially through the debt lever.

This was the first step in what was to become something unanticipated, a concentration of land in private estates, capped by the Roman *latifundia* plantations which, as Pliny decried, became the ruin of Rome. Landlessness became a general social phenomenon. Economic order was replaced by chaos, at least temporarily, for debtors could not earn their way out of debt simply by working harder. Interest rates of 33 % per year quickly increased the debt principal even further beyond the already strapped debtor's ability to pay, doubling his burden in just three years.

Appropriation of the land started with incursions at the very top of the social pyramid, by the royal family and their allies. The first lands to be taken over were those which yielded the largest economic surplus, starting with those belonging to the temples (and of course the palace itself, which rulers turned into their own personal estate). These lands already were organized to provide a regular usufruct. Hitherto used to support administrative and workshop labour, this now was taken by administrators in their private capacity.

Officials in the royal bureaucracy used their position as tax or fee collectors to establish credit claims on those who fell into arrears. Unlike the palace rulers, the object of acquisition by these officials was primarily the subsistence-land of smaller cultivators. The object was to squeeze these lands to generate the same kind of *rentier* surplus and, in time, a body of dispossessed and hence dependent clients which was being created in the public sector.

Fiscal crises accompanying the concentration of wealth

Anthropologists have shown that in pre-monetary economies, the surplus took the form of labour services or the provision of food and other materials that were essential for the performance of public service. Mesopotamia's agrarian societies financed the public sphere out of surplus income generated from land, that is, its *rent*.

The first step taken by the privatizers was to keep the surplus crops for themselves rather than turning them over to the palace. They also appropriated the labour of their debtors, rather than letting cultivators perform their civic *corvée* labour or even military duties. It was indeed this labour that the land appropriators wanted most of all, for it was needed to cultivate the land at harvest-time. Quite simply, the new landlords resented seeing the palace finance public services out of the rent of "their" land. Having obtained this land, they sought to make it exempt from taxes and communal labour obligations.

Increasingly, creditors coveted their debtors' land. However, without labour to cultivate it, this land would not be of much use. There was as yet no supply of "free" labour for hire, that is, economically unfree labour dispossessed of its own land. This fact obliged creditors to leave their debtors and their families in place on the land.

This meant depriving the palace of the community's traditional obligation to provide contingents of fighting men. Accordingly, rulers fought this privatization. By restoring order, cancelling the debts, returning the land to its cultivator-occupants and freeing the debt-bondsmen, they not only restored their army, but in the process blocked an independent oligarchic power from emerging which, in classical Greece and Rome, would succeed in overthrowing the kings and substituting their own, more narrowminded authority.

The spread of unproductive interest-bearing rural debt

Organized warfare drove subsistence cultivators into the arms of creditors. Most of these were officials in the royal bureaucracy; others were heiresses, whose families had placed them in temple complexes to invest the family money rather than marry and convey their dowries out of their clan. Still other creditors were merchants, who accumulated money through foreign trade, or war chieftains building up claims for payment on their clients.

What all these creditors had in common was a desire for collateral as security for their financial claims. Sometimes they accepted family-members as pledges; indeed, this debt bondage was civilization's first form of dependent able-bodied labour. (Wage labour would take centuries longer to develop, and seems to have developed first for mercenaries and seasonal agricultural workers.) In the end, creditors took their gains in the form of foreclosure on the property and enslaving their debtors.

The new property rights were rights of permanent eviction and expropriation. In legal language, these rights displaced rights of person.

What Roman (and hence, modern) law called "security of tenure" actually was tenurial chaos, from the vantage point of ancient traditions of social survival and equity. Privatization of the land also deprived the community of its rights to the economic surplus for use in socially necessary ways. What modern economic terminology calls "market freedom" thus connoted the right of property to deprive the weaker members of society of their own freedom-of-person, and society at large of its freedom of economic self-determination and even economic survival.

Failure periodically to restore economic order by proclaiming Clean Slates

The Sumerian economic planners who innovated the charging of land-rent and interest back in the third millennium BC hardly intended this outcome. What they sought was a means to support the public infrastructure, which they organized in the first instance as temple corporations. These were history's first business corporations. It is in them that one finds the first organization of dependent ration (proto-wage) labour, professional administrators and their account-keeping, land-rent to support these personnel, standardized prices, weights and measures, annual reports, and even yearend annual meetings with their grand banquets, replete with the presentation of audited accounts.

As the commercial practices which the temples developed came to be emulated by private individuals acting on their own account, rulers sought to correct matters by proclaiming Clean Slates. These restored popular rights to the means of livelihood to counteract personal debt and privatization of the land. Agrarian debts were abolished and bondservants were freed when new rulers took the throne or "proclaimed order" for immediate civic reasons.

For thousands of years, communities had erected sanctions to protect personal land rights. The reason was self-evident. Societies were not yet rich enough to support displaced cultivators on welfare. Each family had to support itself. This meant supporting oneself on the land, on one's own plot with one's own animals. These assets accordingly were made immune from seizure.

One way to protect personal right-of-access to the land was to limit its alienation, that is, its sale (usually at a distress price) or the practice of pledging it for debt and subsequently forfeiting it. Public laws nullified such sales or forfeitures "below the full price," e.g. by pledging land-rights as collateral for a loan at only a fraction of the land's full value (in an epoch when land prices stood at only one to three times annual rent). Another sanction decreed that the land could be conveyed only to one's heirs.

In the face of Mesopotamian rulers restoring order by proclaiming Clean Slates, creditors began to devise loopholes (and this in an epoch when *lawyers* had not yet become a profession; that would arise only in Rome). The Babylonians (and even more so the Nuzians, upstream along the Euphrates) developed the legal loophole of false adoptions. The debtor would adopt his creditor as his heir, to the exclusion of his own children. Creditors also forced their debtors to sign a waiver of their rights to recover the land under royal Clean Slate proclamations. Rulers declared such waivers to be illegal, but access to royal justice often ran by way of the local headmen who themselves were the offending parties!

After Babylonia fell to foreign occupiers after 1595 BC, these Clean Slate edicts stopped. As the military burden grew heavier, more people lost their land to foreclosing creditors. To compensate for this state of affairs, the new landowners were expected to become patrons to the clients they had dispossessed. Thus was created the culture of dependency which, a millennium later, would find its epitome in Rome.

But by this time, rulers had long been displaced by aristocracies who permanently blocked any attempts to restore order on earth. The idea became otherworldly, being postponed until the Day of Judgment.

The social impact of debt and privatization of the land
Starting in Babylonian times after about 2000 BC, in what archaeologists call the Middle Bronze Age, the seemingly intractable problems of the modern era appear as part and parcel of the privatization syndrome: conflicts between creditors and debtors over possession of the land, and a deepening impoverishment of economies locked in a spiral of indebtedness mounting up in excess of the capacity to pay. Poverty became a systematic element of normal everyday life as people were deprived of the ability to earn their bread.

Hunger, no longer a random result of inclement weather, became an inevitability. Uprooted families who had lost their lands to foreclosing creditors sought whatever livelihood they could find. Many joined roving bands to find whatever seasonal harvesting or other work was available. Many ended up as mercenaries, or becoming predators on their own, such as the *hapiru* bands attested in the Levant ca. 1400 BC. This creation of a dispossessed labour force became another defining characteristic of our civilization. It signifies the origin of dependent labour-for-hire.

Private appropriation of the land, especially by erstwhile public officials and military commanders, was aggravated by the devastation of warfare, alien overlordship, and domestic monopolization of the land by local puppets of the foreign chieftains. This fragmentation of society into hierarchies based on the monopoly of land, a class-based tool to subordinate people to the new landlord elite, became yet another defining characteristic of civilization.

The nexus of warfare, rising rural indebtedness, fiscal strangulation resulting from private individuals appropriating the land (and taking the surplus that hitherto had accrued to the public sector), and indeed, the increasing polarization of landownership patterns, has wielded a fateful influence to this day. One professor of history has summarized Britain's experience during the century leading up to the industrial revolution in these terms:

> Wars were never cheap, but they were fought over such a span that they became progressively more costly. Government both borrowed and taxed to finance them. It borrowed so heavily that the greater part of its peacetime revenue was mortgaged to service and repay its debt. Financing the industrial revolution was small beer compared with the cost of waging war. In 1785 it cost £63,174 to build the 100-gun ship *Victory*. That was five times greater than the fixed capital value of Ambrose Crawley's celebrated iron works – one of the industrial wonders of the age.[2]

Instead of serving the interests of its citizens, the state in 18th-century Britain, found itself locked into a vicious fiscal circle.

> Only a modest proportion of government expenditure went on civil matters, while between 75 and 85 per cent of annual expenditure went either on current spending on the Army, Navy and ordnance, or else to the service of war debts. Wars became ever more expensive, and with them the national debt rose to heights that to contemporaries seemed awesome.[3]

The resulting fiscal knot has been tightened around the necks of citizens in the kind of spiral that systems analysts call positive feedback: war *results in* private debts *results in* inability of the private sector to support the public sector *results in* increased taxation or public debt *results in* more borrowing to pay the interest on public debts. And: creation of a warlord aristocracy *results in* privatization of the commons *results in* landlessness and a loss of the means for self-support for a growing proportion of the population *results in* dependency on servile or wage labour, or on charity, culminating most recently in the welfare state which threatens to become a fiscal Leviathan in its own right — once again, inequitably benefiting the Few at the expense of the Many.

The Welfare State
There is now sufficient evidence to indicate that electorates have come to view the welfare state as a failure. It certainly is not what liberals and socialists campaigned for a century ago. Over the past hundred years the material conditions have improved for the population *on average*, but in Dr. Miller's view, that improvement should not be attributed to the welfare state. It would have happened anyway, through the hard work and capital accumulation of the last four generations of workers.

The test to which Dr. Miller subjects the welfare state is a fair one. Taking Britain as his case study, he explores the question of whether government intervention through the public sector improved the relative position of those who were at the bottom of the social scale in the 19th century. The answer is unambiguous: No! The luck of the demographic and hereditary dice has more influence than the law of the land. Each year over 40,000 deaths occur among people who would continue to live if they had been born into professional families. Each year more than 3,000 infants die because they had the hard luck to be born to parents who do not count as professionals.

Assuming that an infant survives his bad luck of being born to lower-class parents, he then suffers from an injustice that persists throughout his life. For although he may save money for his pension to finance the comforts of old age, he stands a poor chance of enjoying the benefits of the sacrifices of his lifetime. For as a member of the working class, he faces a shorter life span than that of professionals: five years may be cut off his life. For these people it really is not worth saving up for old age; they do not live to enjoy the benefits.

Dr. Miller, who undertakes research for the General Medical Council at the Wolfson Institute of Preventive Medicine based in The Medical College of St. Bartholomew's Hospital, London, is not hostile to the goals of the welfare state:

> In questioning the record of the welfare state, I am not out of sympathy with its basic tenets. I am diametrically opposed to Thatcherism, which espouses the virtues of the Victorian capitalist ethos and sees the welfare state as not merely ineffectual but as dissipative if not actually ruinous. To me, the welfare state is an acknowledgement of the need to reform the capitalist system as it had evolved up to the beginning of this century. My argument is that though reforms were most certainly needed, the welfare approach adopted has been largely ineffectual. The Victorian problems that the welfare state was meant to remedy are still there; the Thatcherites pretend they never existed.[4]

There are many ways in which the statistics demonstrate that little progress has been made over the past hundred years. One of these relates to the physical condition of young Englishmen. A century ago, in the 1890s, the government became alarmed about the poor physique of recruits who were needed for the Boer War. Something had to be done to strengthen the nation's fighting men. A Royal Commission was established to investigate the facts and propose remedies. A century later, and despite the cradle-to-grave welfare services – from the state provision of milk to new approaches in housing and care for the aged – we now find that the army is turning away up to 40% of potential recruits because they are "too weedy."[5]

The welfare state did not and could not succeed, for it was not designed to remodel the foundations of society. Failure therefore continues to pile upon failure. If society is to restore order, it is necessary to recognise the need for a fresh start. What lawmakers now need to do is to define the terms for a new national Clean Slate.

The need for a fresh start
That our social system is grinding to a dead stop is confirmed by the governments of the world's richest nations. They are reconciled to the prospect that once the recession of the 1990s is over (imagining it to be self-

curing, and hence, merely temporary, rather than recognizing it for what it really is – the painfully slow process of the debt-strangulation), millions of people will be without jobs. In a report to its 25 member governments, the Organisation for Economic Co-operation and Development concluded that unemployment would traumatise 35 million people in 1995, and that "not too much should be expected from cyclical recovery, particularly in Europe."

> Unemployment is probably the most widely feared phenomenon of our times. It touches all parts of society. There are 35 million people unemployed in OECD countries. Perhaps another 15 million have either given up looking for work or unwillingly accepted a part-time job. As many as a third of young workers in some OECD countries have no job.[6]

The social implications were not lost on the OECD's Paris-based secretariat, which warned that this unemployment "represents an enormous waste of human resources, reflects an important amount of inefficiency in economic systems, and causes a disturbing degree of social distress."[7] The political and global implications of mass unemployment also were noted:

> It brings with it unravelling of the social fabric, including a loss of authority of the democratic system, and it risks resulting in the disintegrations of the international trading system.[8]

Capitalism relies for its survival on the ability to create and replicate wealth. Today, this ability is being undermined by the *rentier* privatization syndrome inherited from pre-capitalist economic formations as a genetic blot. If today's welfare capitalism is excluding more and more people from work, it is largely because of a carryover of financial and land-tenure characteristics that are antecedent to capitalism. Not only does capitalism not inherently need a parasitic debt overhead and private monopolization of natural and public resources, but these phenomena are actively threatening to destroy it.

The basic question is thus what *kind* of capitalism are we to have? The debt overhead and natural-resource monopoly threaten to bring down our particular economic system, as they did the Roman imperial system and Babylonian public enterprise two thousand years prior to the collapse of the Roman Empire. But need these dynamics bring *us* down too?

Even our medical and demographic breakthroughs are being transformed by the economic overhead problem, by the practice of funding retirement pensions, Social Security and medical insurance via financial savings and their corresponding debt-claims that have the effect of shrinking the economy's ability to support these functions. The irony is that as people live longer, they increase their retirement savings, Social Security and medical claims on those fortunate enough to remain in work. Under these conditions the social contract becomes increasingly unenforceable. A shrinking employed labour force is obliged to support a growing pyramid of retired, geriatric, medical, welfare and other demographic overheads, while the exponentially growing debt overhead creates a financial and real-estate bubble. The result is an artificial hothouse brand of postindustrialism run wildly off course.

The risks of the welfare state have been recognized formally by governments from Britain to the Americas, which have cut back on the provision of welfare services to the population at large even while increasing guarantees and socializing the risks for large institutional investors, de-taxing the land for the benefit of real-estate developers, picking up the "external" costs of improving their property, and cleaning up the ecological mess they have left so that they can recover all their capital (and indeed, capital gains) and proceed to repeat their economic devastation elsewhere.

Britain and America have not been able to formulate better solutions mainly because they limit the analysis of the problem to an obsolete paradigm of property and tax rights. The guiding ideology restricts the range of policy options to those that are favoured by the polluters, the land owners and strip miners, the mineral and oil companies, deforestation companies, and the banks which finance their activities to convert their land-rent into a securitized flow of interest revenue.

Perhaps the time has come to learn the lesson from the clay tablets, glazed cones, buried figurines and public statues on which the Sumerian rulers inscribed their Clean Slate proclamations. What links their epoch to ours are phenomena that warp today's economic functioning as deeply as it did that of the Bronze Age and classical antiquity: debt, land monopolization and tax avoidance by landholders, which undermined social solvency for private benefit.

Our specifically modern problem is the tendency for debt liabilities – and this means, on the asset side of the balance sheet, the economy's savings –

(very diff. sentence.

to accrue interest more rapidly than can be supported by growth in the capacity to pay out of current income and wealth levels. One way or another, the stresses generated by those debts have to be resolved. The question is, how will this resolution occur? By a slow bankruptcy grinding the entire economy to a halt after first having transferred public and private assets into the hands of creditors? Or by deliberately letting the bad debts go (along with their counterpart savings), and re-starting the economy financially and fiscally afresh with an Economic Miracle such as that which triggered postwar Germany's recovery in 1947, when the Allied Powers cancelled all internal German debts and freed the nation from foreign reparations debts?

The Sumerian rulers were anything but irresponsible. The mathematics underlying their economic models were more sophisticated than those of today, for they did not shy away from recognizing the exponential growth of debt at annual rates of 20% or 33 %, in contrast to the slower growth (or even shrinkage) in the means to pay. The edicts of Sumerian and Babylonian rulers show that they recognized the classical distinction between productive and unproductive debt. They neither cancelled commercial silver-debts nor rescued entrepreneurs from their misadventures, but only cancelled consumer barley-debts. They left urban real-estate intact as part of the economic surplus, while restoring popular economic freedom in the form of personal rights to the means of self-support. Thus, what they cancelled were only corrosive creditor claims on land-rights in excess of the capacity to pay.

Unfortunately, the spirit of periodic economic renewal has become a relic of the past. By classical antiquity, dreams of periodic economic renewal, freedom from debt and recovery of the land from its expropriators became otherworldly and utopian, no longer a practical social program but one that was put off to the Millennium, the Day of Judgment at the end of history.

Time and again during the past four thousand years, societies have found themselves crippled by the consequences of the failure to develop rational principles of land tenure and public finance. Time and again, rulers and governments restored social stability by restoring the traditional economic order with its rights of person. But time and again these fresh starts proved unsustainable. The same social activities have repeatedly tightened the noose around people on the land and in the towns, who wanted nothing more than to be left alone to get on with their lives.

The archaeological record throws important light on the character of social disharmony through the ages. It shows that the first to prey upon private lives and encroach on living standards are political leaders operating from within the public sector. The fiscal system becomes a means to reinforce the power of emerging land-rich creditor elites. Rather than rulers restoring equity and spurring enterprise, they become chairmen and prime beneficiaries of the new privatizations, until finally their entire society succumbs to internal debt and land parasitism.[9]

This pattern of development needs a distracting ideology to make what is bad appear good. That is where contemporary economics comes in, as a public-relations front, calling such financial destruction by other names, by euphemisms such as the "postindustrial society."

Beyond the Clean Slate
So deep is the modern world's economic quandary that it needs more than just a fresh start. It needs a philosophy for a fair society.

Simply to cancel debts outright would leave most property in the hands of real-estate developers, joyfully freed of all debt encumbrances. It would make them the richest class in society, unparalleled lords of the earth. Plutarch makes this clear in describing the "wrong" way to cancel debts in his biography of Sparta's reformer-kings of the third century BC, Agis and Cleomenes, as well as their successor, Nabis.

Central to a fair political philosophy is the need to keep the land from reverting into the hands of land-monopolists and creditors. Land and other natural resources must be treated fairly for public revenue purposes. Public resources would revert to the public domain, to be auctioned on fair terms for development and the revenues treated as income, thereby reducing the need to tax labour and physical capital.

Henceforth, what is to be taxed is unearned income – economic parasitism – not productive enterprise. Society would actively shape the marketplace within which enterprise operates, steering it in the direction of the mutual benefit of both the private and public interest rather than to serve *rentier* interests.

The reconstruction of political economy

The 19th-century moral philosophers who developed the concepts and theories that formed the building blocks of political economy viewed their discipline as a social science. Tax policy was central, along with the advocacy of productive rather than unproductive activity. With this fiscal focus and economic growth in mind, political economy became a method to analyze how wealth-producing nations distributed income among their factors of production, and whether these factors consumed or invested the money they earned.[10]

A shortcoming of this approach was the inadequate attention it paid to *rentier* elements. In retrospect this failure is hardly surprising. David Ricardo was the leading bond-broker of his day. His broker's-eye view of the world found debt to be only a means of financing growth, not an economic burden. His adversary, Thomas Robert Malthus, defended landlords as helping to solve rather than causing society's economic problems. Under the influence of these two men, economics evolved with a bias in favour of *rentier* propaganda. And with the establishment of modern-day business schools, well subsidized by the economy's increasingly powerful *rentier* interests, this blind spot has increased.

The neo-classical counter-revolution at the turn of the 20th century blurred the distinctions which classical economists had drawn between land and capital, and between the private and public sectors. This fatally compromised the analysis of economic problems, by urging governments to provide welfare in such a way as to consolidate the power of the very parties that were undermining the capacity to create general prosperity in the first place.

Economists should have explained that the most efficient system of public finance is that which encourages new investment of capital and upgrading of labour, while limiting parasitic *rentier* income and related economic overhead. This is best done by treating the rent of land and other monopoly gains as public revenue, while channeling credit into productive activity, which was the thesis most energetically articulated by American social reformer Henry George. Instead, the neo-classical economists gave their blessing to the growing debt and land-rent overhead, and refused to acknowledge that any given way of making money was more economically productive than any other!

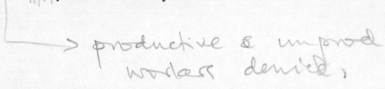

> productive & unprod.
> workers denied,

This bad advice followed naturally from the demise of classical economics and the emphasis it had placed on the unearned character of land-rent. The academic debate concerning public finance was restricted to whether to raise or lower existing tax rates on income indiscriminately, without regard for whether it is earned productively or parasitically. Today's economists no longer acknowledge land-rent's role as a natural source of public taxation – an understanding which, in modern times, originated with the French Physiocrats and was refined from Adam Smith through David Ricardo, John Stuart Mill and Alfred Marshall. Although this perception is cursorily confirmed in some textbooks, and even acknowledged freely by many Nobel laureates, it is a taboo subject when it comes to formulating policies to deal with today's exploding budget deficits.[11]

Operating seemingly within conventional paradigms, the New Right empowered by Ronald Reagan and Margaret Thatcher were able to drive their nations deeper into debt. Instead of a full wartime mobilization such as historically had been the prime cause of national debts, the new indebtedness stemmed mainly from mushrooming interest payments accruing on the existing stock of debt/saving, coupled with a lessening tax burden on *rentiers*. Instead of being taxed, the latter were given public welfare. The result was a transfer of income and wealth from taxpayers to creditors, to a degree never experienced before in history. The result was an explosion of postindustrial economic parasitism, freed from the regulations and even the taxes that hitherto had held it in check.

In the US, for example, the savings and loan (building society) industry bailout guaranteed depositor claims despite the fact that these were secured by bad real-estate speculation. Indeed, the worse the mismanagement, the higher the interest received by money managers as compensation for their "risk" – one that the government picked up *in toto*, for a final bill that will amount to somewhere between $1 and $1.5 trillion.

Paying off these financial claims is a burden that now weighs upon the back of corporate capital as well as the labour of taxpayers. Both capital and labour thus are now oppressed by a common *rentier* enemy.

No wonder people have lost the sense of freedom to work. In England, the process began with the uncoupling of culture from the natural environment in the Enclosure movements that inaugurated the modern industrial epoch. People who lost their access rights to the land were deprived of the basic right to work for themselves. Today, even the prospect of industrial employment is being closed off as debt-ridden economies enter the phase of postindustrialism, a perverse condition in which corporations are so heavily indebted that they only can pay their bondholders, bankers and other creditors by selling off their assets.

Rent: reconnecting people to land and the environment

The need to refocus policy in the direction of social harmony and economic efficiency will not be easy, psychologically, because we are burdened with a great deal of historical baggage. The problem has now assumed global proportions. Through colonisation, Europe – led by Britain and Holland – infected much of the world with the privatisation syndrome. As the Europeans expanded into Africa, Asia and Latin America, they co-opted local chiefs as their agents. The usual ploy was to register all land-rights in their names and then "negotiate" with them to alienate these rights to the colonising powers or pledge them for debt, while taxing their own peoples to build the ports, transport infrastructure, power plants and related activities associated with these plantation, forestry, mineral and oil industries. Finally, they had to tax yet more to clean up after these foreign investors had left, as well as to provide soldiers for the colonising power's armies.

Britain had incorporated the rogue genes into her social system during the Middle Ages. Following the departure of the imperial Roman centurions, the Anglo-Saxons had developed a social relationship with land based on use-rights which ensured a coherent relationship between society and nature. Rent revenues formed the prime source of public revenue. However, the invasions of Viking and Norman overlords brought a new feudal aristocracy, sanctified by the Roman church and soon thrown as prey to the Italian bankers portrayed so scathingly in Dante's *Inferno* and Matthew Paris's *Annals*.

Sir Kenneth Jupp, who served for 15 years as a judge in the English High Court,[12] has described how the newcomers took possession of the land by transferring rights formerly associated with people to landed property itself – that is, to its absentee appropriators rather than its users – and thereby skilfully casting aside the old reciprocal obligations associated with this property. The shift suited a small class of people who became Lords of the Land, and hence Masters of the People.

As a result of this privatisation of rights to the benefits of land, there developed personal rights to charge others for the use of what originally had been their own holding by communal right as citizens. People were forced to depend for their lives not on their own labours or the bountifulness of nature, but on the whims of the new – and, as every Irishman knows, alien – lords of the land.

The new property rights conferred an unprecedented power to exclude people from access to the land. The outcasts made up a growing proportion of the population. Their ranks even included war veterans, who since antiquity had received special protection by being assured their own settlement plots in gratitude for their public service. Henceforth, they were expelled from the land and turned into loom-fodder.

The history of civilization and its ultimate political achievement, the nation-state protecting land and resource ownership by the few, as a lever to be turned against the many, was an inversion of the archaic natural order. The process must now be put into reverse, by a new Clean Slate proclamation linked with a radical reform that neutralizes the rogue genes in our culture.

This strong, literally millennarist response reflects the degree to which today's economic problems have reached a historically unique scale. For one thing, the global character of today's crisis necessitates such a qualitative change. What hitherto was merely national decadence today becomes a worldwide Super Decadence. Now that we live in One World, interdependency magnifies every shock to the social system, leaving no region untouched.

Never before have so many countries recognised the need for a fresh start to wipe the slate clean. It is obvious that the existing level of debt cannot be paid off. Attempts to do so will merely strip debtor countries of their remaining public wealth, dooming them to IMF austerity and more World Bank-sponsored asset-stripping.

Peoples ranging from Russia in the north to Africa at the end of the southern hemisphere have swept away Stalinist communism on the one hand and apartheid capitalism on the other. They are now searching for new social models. The question is whether they will improve on the past, or incorporate its surviving *rentier* genes into their economic reordering. Will they see how narrowminded is the advice being cooked up by the teams of World Bank and IMF advisors? Will they truly break new ground? Or will they fail to imagine a better world and to fight to create a more independent economy?

These countries writing new constitutions afford the rest of us the opportunity to see the possibility of redefining the rights of men and women in a new natural order. This opportunity was last experienced 200 years ago, during what the outcasts had hoped would be the popular revolutions of France and America. However, the constitution-makers will fail again if they do not bring to bear a deeper understanding of how society works. This time they must avoid privatizing the land, taxing the smaller holders while giving special breaks to the large land monopolists and, ultimately, to their creditors.[13]

The contributors to the present series of books believe that if culture is to evolve in the direction of a sustainable solution, we need to focus attention on the failures of taxation and on economic parasitism, above all debt-parasitism and absentee landlordship that society's accumulated savings are now busy financing across the face of our planet. We need a system of public finance that recognises the principles of social equity and environmental responsibility embedded in our primordial land ethic.

Modern – or rather, contemporary – social science has no ready-made analytic model to place at our disposal. Economics has become particularly banal by insisting that land and other natural resources (along with other natural monopolies) are not distinctively important, but merely normal modes of wealth-seeking, not to be taxed differently from other modes. Debt financing is viewed merely as a form of funding the creation of wealth, not as an intrusive economic overhead. Indeed, the GNP format for national income accounting draws no distinction between wealth and overhead, between productive and parasitic economic activity.

These harmful failures to distinguish between the economically good and bad have become the very foundation of the self-proclaimed "generality" of today's economics. The disengagement of economics from its classical foundations – the unearthing of economic theory, one might say – began a century ago and can be traced through the statements of such Nobel laureates as James Buchanan, who asserts that "in centuries past, 'land,' as such, was far more important, relatively, than it is today."[14]

The Georgist paradigm

The model we offer as a tool for analysis is named after the American social reformer Henry George (1839-97). Why Henry George? Leo Tolstoy offers a good reason that remains as valid today as when it was written a century ago:

> The evolution of man's knowledge in reference to the use of land goes on, and . . . the process of putting this thought into action must soon commence. In these processes . . . Henry George was and is the pioneer and leader of the movement. Herein his paramount importance rests. He has, by his excellent works, materially contributed both to the improving of people's ideas on this question as well as to their direction on a practical basis.[15]

Henry George offered his ideas on social reform in *Progress and Poverty* (1879), which quickly became the target of a well-subsidized vituperative attack by academic economists.[16] In his subsequent *Social Problems* (1884) as well as in his journalism, George dealt with the problems of public debts and what he rightly called the "fictitious capital" which established parasitic claims on society's wealth-producing activities.

The authors of the volumes in The Georgist Paradigm series build on the problem-solving principles articulated by Henry George to help governments visualise how, in the 21st century, they may succeed in creating a fair society where their predecessors failed. Without such a new approach, politicians will continue to lead people into the traps that found their origin in Mesopotamia. So our starting point has to be the recognition that rent-taking and the debt overhead and resource monopolization does not herald a new post-industrial society. Rather, it constitutes economic obsolescence through self-cannibalization, a fate from which we can liberate ourselves by adopting the fiscal principles embedded in the Georgist paradigm.

Footnotes

1 "Early wars (in the sense of organized struggles) appear to have occurred in the area now known loosely as the Middle East and came about due to geography. In about 5000 BC, people known as Sumerians occupied the area called the Plain of Shinar, and this fertile region became the envy of surrounding desert and mountain tribes." Arthur Banks, *A World Atlas of*

Military History, Vol.1, London: Seeley Service, 1973, p.3.

2 John Rule, *The Vital Century: England's Developing Economy, 1714-1815*, London: Longman, 1992, p.276.

3 *Ibid.*, citing J. Brewer, *The Sinews of Power*, London: Unwin, 1989.

4 G.J. Miller, "Verdict on the Welfare State", *Land & Liberty*, London, July-August 1994.

5 Charles Hymas and Annabel Heseltine, "Army forced to turn away teenage weeds", *The Sunday Times*, London, July 19, 1994.

6 *The OECD Jobs Study*, Paris: OECD, 1994, p.7.

7 *Ibid.*, p.9.

8 *Ibid.*, p.29.

9 The contemporary evidence from the United States is spelt out in the study by two investigative reporters from *The Philadelphia Enquirer*. Donald L. Barlett and James B. Steele, in *America: Who Really Pays the Taxes?* (New York: Simon & Schuster, 1994) show that there are two streams of taxation, one for the rich, the other for the poor. Income earners interviewed by the journalists had pointed to a tax system that was "perceived to be unfair, a system that they believed was contributing to their falling standard of living, accelerating the drift toward inequality, and eroding the essential trust between citizen and government" (*ibid.*, p.5). This picture is confirmed by the evidence on the tax burden and income distribution in Britain.

10 Adam Smith can be criticized for his willingness to adopt a theory of property rights congenial to his class. Nonetheless, he did develop the concepts of public finance which did challenge the financial interests of landowners. See Fred Harrison, *The Power in the Land*, London: Shepheard Walwyn, 1983, Ch.22.

11 This criticism of economics cannot be directed at other disciplines, which have begun to integrate land into their models. Archaeology is an interesting example. Over 20 years ago, archaeologists acknowledged that "It is only when excavated material is considered in relation to the resources of the territory utilized [land], the nature of the technology [capital] and the size of the community [labour], that a meaningful picture is likely to emerge of the manner in which economic needs were met". Grahame Clark, "Foreword", in E.S. Higgs, *Papers in Economic Prehistory*, Cambridge: The University Press, 1972, p.ix.

12 Kenneth Jupp, in Ronald Banks and Kenneth Jupp (editors), *Private Property and Public Finance*, London: Shepheard-Walwyn/CIT, 1995.

13 The constitutional errors that have crippled the United States are outlined by Fred Harrison in *The Corruption of Economics*, London: Shepheard-Walwyn/CIT, 1994.

14 James M. Buchanan, *The Public Finances*, Homewood, Ill.: Richard D. Irwin, 1960, p.440. A critique that begins to restore the primacy of land is offered by Mason Gaffney, a professor of economics at the University of California. See especially his contribution to *Land and Taxation* (1994).

15 Letter from Leo Tolstoy to Bernard Eulenstein, cited in "Count Tolstoi on Henry George", *The Single Tax*, Glasgow, July 1894, p.3.

16 See especially Mason Gaffney's analysis of the behaviour of some of the most influential neo-classical economists in *The Corruption of Economics*.

Land Monopolization, Fiscal Crises and Clean Slate "Jubilee" Proclamations in Antiquity

Michael Hudson

his essay compares Middle Bronze Age Mesopotamia (2000-1600
BC), classical antiquity (750 BC-300 AD) and the Byzantine
Empire (330-1204 AD) to trace the corrosive dynamics of debt,
absentee land-ownership, monopolization and economic polarization. The
interaction of these influences has destroyed societies repeatedly throughout
history. The lesson to be learned is that private possession of communal
land rights threw off its originally public context, undercutting society's
economic viability again and again, to the point where it has destroyed
entire civilizations.

This historical overview provides a basic insight into the origins of
today's economic crisis. Debt overhead once again is transferring real
estate and farms, natural resources (oil, other minerals and forest products),
industry and government-owned assets into the hands of a narrowing layer
of bankers, bondholders and other creditors. The concentration of land and
natural resource rights into ever fewer hands is part of a longer historical
process in which private investment has been at the expense of the public
interest.

Over the past century a major field for finance capital has been the
creation of railroads and exploitation of natural resources. In both cases
such capital has negotiated special tax breaks that have involved the
hoarding of land. The oil industry's international depletion allowance and
low royalty payments at subsidized rates on public lands are the most
notorious examples. Tax breaks for mining, real-estate depreciation and
the interest payments are equally serious concessions. The upshot is to tax

the rest of the public to create transport, water and other public infrastructure to enhance the value of private holdings. Meanwhile, the money for this public spending is borrowed at interest, burdening taxpayers with higher costs to facilitate these giveaways to special interests.

This has been the essence of monopoly power throughout history - and also the essence of hyperinflations. Matters have become especially pronounced in third world countries, whose regimes have come under life-or-death pressure from the International Monetary Fund and World Bank, backed by the U.S. and European governments, to provide special concessions to foreign investors in an attempt to generate more foreign exchange. Instead of being invested productively, this money is used merely to service existing foreign debts and facilitate capital flight to offshore havens, from which the money is recycled into the North American and European banking systems. The result has left ostensibly resource-rich countries in debt beyond their capacity to pay, creating a permanent fiscal and foreign-exchange crisis.

At least antiquity's governments were not debtors; typically they were creditors. Industry was not financed by debt; it was self-sustaining, as Moses Finley has demonstrated so strongly. But these conditions no longer are true, making the crisis all the more serious. A contrast between ancient and modern modes of public and private finance may provide a deeper understanding of the economic and fiscal drama now being enacted, and help show both good and bad ways that societies have chosen to resolve their debt, land-tenure and tax problems.

Public obligations owed by landed property-holders, above all for military service (and for the performance of corvée labor in the Near East), have a pedigree going back at least to Sumerian times in the third millennium BC. Almost as old is the striving by rich and powerful families to avoid such obligations on their own holdings. Prior to the development of a land market, large holdings were built up mainly by foreclosing on subsistence lands pledged by insolvent debtors.

The transfer of these hitherto communally allocated subsistence lands to large property owners helped consolidate hereditary aristocracies and oligarchies to the point where their own power was able to undercut that of centralized authority. The ensuing privatization of economic power - and its associated displacement of rights-of-person by property rights - was achieved by strangling governments fiscally and militarily, leading to political and economic collapse. This essay accordingly discusses the earliest documented examples in the Old Babylonian period (1800-1600 BC), and sketches the subsequent dynamic of economic polarization down through the Roman *latifundia* to Byzantium.

I
Bronze Age

Mikhail Rostovtzeff (1926) has provided the classic description of how, during the early centuries of our modern era, Rome's wealthiest landowning families managed to throw taxes onto the classes below them. This prevented any "middle class" of "yeomanry" from emerging out of the ranks of the *curialis* class. Much the same phenomenon is found in the East Roman (Byzantine) empire from the 9th through 11th centuries. In England, warlord Norman kings parcelled out the land in huge tracts to their companions and barons in exchange for the latter providing money and services, only to see this reciprocity of obligations cut away by the Magna Carta in 1215, by the Uprising of the Barons in 1258-65, by the enclosure movements, and by the Glorious Revolution of 1688. Today, large developers in many cities and countries typically are reimbursed for their campaign contributions by receiving tax breaks for their property.

Internationally, repressive regimes gain support by turning over mineral and land rights to foreigners, while running into debt to build infrastructure to speed the process of denuding their forests, depleting their soil and mines, shifting the land from producing domestic food grains to export crops, and leaving holes in the ground where their national patrimony once lay - while taxing local populations to provide the roads, port facilities and cleanup costs needed to provide these to investors at as low a cost as possible, so as to provide as large a surplus as possible, to be capitalized as a basis for borrowing the money to set the process in motion. This is the strategy of international finance capital and the industries and agribusiness it has drawn into its sway.

36

In each society the winning of tax-exemption by well-placed landholders and natural-resource appropriators appears as a singular, nearly accidental result of jockeying for position, but looking over the broad sweep of history, a common pattern emerges spanning over four thousand years, extending back to the Middle Bronze Age, 2000-1600 BC. Typically a politically weak ruler is confronted with a strong aristocratic leader mobilizing the leading families behind him. Mesopotamian rulers countered this by periodically restoring "economic order," that is, by issuing Clean Slate proclamations, but this practice did not survive into oligarchic Greek and Roman antiquity.

Social functions of archaic land tenure
Self-support was the key to the economic survival of archaic communities. Recognizing this fact, the guiding Bronze Age spirit (dare we say ideology?) was basically one of mutual aid in a militarized context. Citizens were assured the means of self-support on the land in return for providing military service in the draft, often supplemented by various types of seasonal *corvée* labor.

Most tribal and other precommercial land tenure was communally allocated. Citizenship status typically was defined by the allotment of land rights so as to enable citizens to support their families. The objective was not anything so modern as to enable citizens to make money by leasing out the land for rent, much less to exploit it commercially by hiring landless cultivators. Certainly the aim was not to transfer land into the hands of absentee buyers. Rather, the objective was largely military. Armies were composed of all able adult males from the landed families. In addition to their military role, their labor might be requisitioned for communal tasks such as building dikes or harvesting grain on public lands. Newcomers, refugees seeking asylum, and the growing domestic population were either provided with their own land, or became dependents in the households of landholding families, or had to emigrate to colonial offshoots (typically after serving in the army to obtain veteran status).

Archaic communities restricted the sale or forfeiture of subsistence landholdings in order to preserve self-sufficiency for their members. Selling one's land, or even borrowing against it, impaired the ability of citizens to perform their communal duties, for it meant a loss of self-support. Archaic interest rates were beyond the ability of many debtors to keep up with, and property once mortgaged was often lost. This is why Mesopotamian communities, where interest-bearing debt is first attested, long blocked the land from being pledged and forfeited for more than merely temporary duration. If it had to be sold as a result of need, relatives or neighbors typically had the right of first refusal and the sale was only temporary, being subject to redemption. This redeemability sanction preserved land in the hands of local communities and their kinship groupings rather than letting it be forfeited or sold to outsiders, including merchants and royal officials.

Borrowing money to acquire land, the hallmark of modern real-estate development, was unheard of.

How the Sumerians maintained economic balance
Southern Mesopotamian land tenure involved numerous types of property (Diakonoff 1982 provides the classic review). Rural land was allocated to citizens as their means of self-support. Individual lots appear to have been redistributed periodically, normally to the heirs of its customary holders. These lots could be alienated temporarily as pledges for loans or other obligations, or even sold for emergency money, but were expected to be redeemed by the debtor, his relatives or neighbors as soon as economic conditions permitted. Failing such redemption, they were restored to their customary owners when rulers proclaimed "economic order" - *amargi* in Sumerian, *andurarum* in Akkadian and Babylonian, *misharum* in Babylonian, and *shudutu* in Hurrian, culminating in the biblical *deror* legislation of Leviticus 25, popularly known as the Jubilee Year.

Sumerian communities also set aside land in the form of perpetual holdings for their local temples to provide sustenance for their administrators and nonagricultural dependents who could not work in agriculture because of being widowed or orphaned, or because of illness, blindness, birth defects or other infirmities.

Turning over this land, as well as herds of animals and other assets to their city-temples to enable them to be self-supporting was the Sumerian alternative to taxation. These endowments were permanent, making their public holders the first documented landlords, at least in the sense of absentee landlords collecting a net usufruct from the land. These temple and palace lands thus represent history's first documented "permanent" property devoted to producing a regular rent-usufruct. Most of this land was let out on a sharecropping basis, usually via palace managers as middlemen, settling at a third of the crop by the end of the third millennium. Widowed mothers and orphaned children were placed in handicraft workshops to weave textiles for exports or perform other tasks compatible with their infirmities.

Whereas private land transfers were only temporary in duration, land transfers to the public sector were permanent. Temple lands could not be alienated, nor were those of the palaces, which emerged after about 2750 BC in southern Mesopotamia. Palace rulers purchased lands from the communal groupings (as documented for instance in the Stele of Manishtushu in the Akkadian period c. 2250 BC).

Merchants and other well-to-do citizens acquired town-houses, which they could buy or sell freely, including individual floors or rooms, without being subject to any repurchase options or other redistributive measures. Inasmuch as these properties were not part of the subsistence sector, there was no pressing need to redistribute them when rulers "proclaimed order." Their ownership was left intact, as were commercial silver-debts as opposed to consumer barley-debts. The overall economy thus was allowed to grow, while taking measures to prevent its wealth from being used in ways that would undercut the rural sector's long-term balance. *Only subsistence lands were protected from permanent alienation, so as to preserve a self-supporting rural population intact alongside a commercial urban economy.*

What concerned rulers was that in addition to being a misfortune for debtors (who typically lost their status as citizens when they lost their land), foreclosures caused fiscal problems for the public sector. Creditors wanted the land's usufruct, often at the expense of the palace in the case of royal sharecropping lands leased in exchange for a third or more of the crop as rent. Debtors were tied to their creditors virtually as servants, and hence were not available for the army or to provide labor services and pay fees.

To rectify this situation, rulers cancelled back taxes and the debts stemming from them, and also reversed the forfeitures of personnel and land to collectors and other creditors. These "restorations of order" were proclaimed at least once each generation, most typically when new rulers took the throne or when they celebrated their thirtieth anniversary of rule, or occasionally as economic and military conditions warranted.

Communal land tenure helped guarantee the supply of labor services to the public sector as part of the reciprocal responsibilities between community members, the palace and its administrative bureaucracy. This reciprocity was interrupted by absentee land acquisition on the part of members of the royal bureaucracy. *Tamkaru* merchants collected taxes and often, in the process, establishing financial claims on community members by paying on their behalf the moneys due - arrears which mounted up at interest.

Military disruption also disturbed the circular flow of products and money. When men were called away from their land to fight, or when fighting devastated the land, some families fell into arrears and ended up pledging their servant girls, children, wives, or cattle to creditors. In time they pledged their lands, or more accurately, their crop usufruct, for until a labor market developed in the second millennium, debtors were left on the land, where they were needed to plant and harvest the crops for their creditors.

The first response of Hammurapi and other Babylonian rulers to the land-foreclosure problem was to proclaim laws preventing creditors from interfering with the "originally" envisioned balanced order. Even more important, they proclaimed *misharum* acts, that is, Clean Slates. These edicts were designed to restore the idealized and symmetrical "straight order," or at least the *status quo ante*, by returning to customary holders the lands that had been forfeited for debt or, what virtually was the same thing, sold below market price.

This put local big-men and other members of Babylonia's royal bureaucracy in their place by taking away the land with which they had aggrandized themselves at the expense of the palace. Many of these lands had been foreclosed in settlement of unpaid tax obligations. Moneys owed by these officials to the palace likewise were annulled, enabling a new, equitable and debt-free fiscal and financial start to be made. This restored the ability of localities to perform the military duties with which they were charged and on which the palace depended.

Public temples as communal corporations

An archaeological review of Bronze Age Mesopotamia throws light on the debate over the "tragedy of the (unmanaged) commons" - the alleged tendency for communalistic forms of property to be unregulated, unmanaged and indeed, unmanageable. Communal resource-users are deemed unable to devise rules to restrain overgrazing on the land and other selfish exploitation of communal resources. A corollary is that communal ownership is not conducive to capital investment.

These ideas, as enunciated by Hardin (1968), have been used to defend the idea of private property's natural superiority. They convey the impression that no workable means have been found to allocate capital expenses communally, even by charging equitable user-fees. Capital improvements on the land, to say nothing of handicraft industry and its workshops, are supposed to be made only by replacing communalist use-rights with a regime of private ownership. A natural selection thus appears to be at work favoring privatization over communalistic modes of property rights in land.

If this idea is wrong, it is wrongheadedness with a political purpose. The purpose is to distract observers' eyes from the inception of economic enterprise in the public sector, starting with the Sumerian temples and palaces. An examination of economic history ranging from 3rd-millennium Sumer through the Byzantine empire reveals the reverse of the Hardin thesis. *Privatized property is what turns out to be unmanageable and inequitable!* In a nutshell, a narrowing layer of landowners and other wealthy families monopolize the economy's wealth and, in the political sphere, divest themselves of fiscal responsibility to contribute to their societies' survival.

"In the beginning," large-scale capital accumulation necessarily was communal, if only because individual families lacked the capital to invest in major undertakings. Starting with the land, this communal investment extended to irrigation systems and the accumulation of herds, culminating in something unprecedented and not subsequently repeated: public-sector investment in handicraft workshops and transport systems (boats, transport canals and donkey caravans). What is remarkable is that this was done in ways that were compatible with personal entrepreneurial drives. Individuals could benefit as temple or palace merchants, collectors and other public positions. Indeed, their opportunities for gain followed mainly from their status as public servants.

This public-sector mode of Sumerian investment has not been more broadly acknowledged mainly because of the political winds of our times. It is ideologically out of favor to notice that the commons almost never are unmanaged, as Hardin (1991) was later to acknowledge. Communal land normally is open only to community members, not to everyone. In exchange for access to land, members traditionally are obliged to provide reciprocal duties to the community, *e.g.* in the form of labor services (both in the military draft and corvée labor) or money to cover the cost of someone else providing these services. They also are obliged to pay user-fees to cover the costs of making capital improvements such as irrigation systems, and for the labor of public professional workers. The organizers of these services in the first instance - and hence, the first recipients of their user-fees - were the temples and palace, not private providers.

Where Sumer went further than, say, medieval England in undertaking public investment was in endowing city-temples and their workshops with capital resources to pursue export production and related commercial surplus-generating activity. Many of the resulting commercial gains were reinvested, making temple (and later, palace) investments the world's major capital accumulations of the Early, Middle and even Late Bronze Age, 3500-1200 BC.

Earlier generations of archaeologists were prevented from recognizing this complex dynamic of public enterprise by their private-enterprise blinders on the one hand, and on the other by the temple-state theory popular in the 1920s, holding that the temples owned all the land. Instead of perceiving Sumer to be the mixed economy that it was, speculation focused on an either/or choice between individualism and nearly despotic statism. Bronze Age Mesopotamia was made to appear as an entirely different continuum (which Marxists called Oriental despotism), not as the inception of western economic civilization and enterprise. Since the 1960s, however, the researches of Igor Diakonoff and Ignace Gelb have shown that communities endowed their temples with land and other resources to undertake large-scale investment as corporately demarcated bodies, set apart to perform particular economic and ceremonial functions, including the first systematic surplus-producing market activities.

Civilization's first formally *economic* investment thus was public. As it became privatized over subsequent centuries - indeed, millennia - the result was not a takeoff as much as it was a descent into anarchy. Once wealth became irreversibly centralized in the hands of the Few, economic polarization destroyed the traditional economic order. Royal restorations of order and equity became a thing of the past. This undercut the archaic social value system based on ideas of righteousness and equity.

Anarchy and corruption are precisely what Hardin and his fellow private-property advocates insist tend to result from communally managed assets. This may seem true of Soviet-type bureaucracies and third-world kleptocracies, but the earliest documented public enterprise had checks and balances to prevent such mismanagement. Indeed, cuneiformists have traced how the inception of writing was developed in response to the need for account-keeping as a check on the behavior of bureaucratic administrators. The auditing of annual balance sheets was part of an institutional complex of practices that included annual meetings and their attendent festivities, the invention of standardized weights and measures, and the standardization of economic phenomena in general, so as to regularize impersonal bulk exchange on equal terms for all buyers and sellers. Uniform rent rates were established, along with interest rates, incomes and professional fees for public occupations (as specified in Hammurapi's laws), and contractual formalities. These economic phenomena mark the watershed beyond the looser, interpersonal ("anthropological") exchange. Products of the explosive flourescence of Mesopotamian public enterprise, they were woven into the economic and social cosmos so smoothly as to become part and parcel of Bronze Age natural law.

This Mesopotamian flourescence brought into being, and legitimized, the social values associated with gain-seeking enterprise. Such enterprise was created on a relatively large scale mainly because it required a quantum leap to establish its new norms. If it began in "households of the gods" rather than in individual households - even those of big-men and chieftains - this was largely because the Bronze Age was still an epoch when well-to-do individuals were expected to be openhanded. They consumed their affluence conspicuously rather than accumulating wealth as a lever to gain yet more wealth, without limit. Social values had not yet developed to the point where community members were willing to permit individuals to disenfranchise citizens by monopolizing subsistence lands and reducing citizens to irredeemable bondage. It was to preserve the functioning of their communities economically intact that rulers regularly reversed private subsistence-land appropriations by "restoring order."

Historians are permitted - are indeed, obliged in the light of today's economic strains - to ask whether the privatization of Bronze Age public enterprise had a salutary effect or contributed to economic devolution and disintegration. Did the emerging class of personal landholders develop a protestant ethic, thereby pulling their civilization ahead to a higher plane? Or, did they indulge themselves in the traditional ethic of conspicuous consumption to the point of interfering with society's economic linkages and basic needs? Did the emerging aristocracies tend to invest their wealth productively, or to sink it into the acquisition of more land and dependent clients, and to indulge in warfare and looting in a drive to gain from foreigners the revenue they no longer could produce at home?

Looking over the economic dynamic emanating from Bronze Age Mesopotamia as constituting a long wave, one can see that *privatizing the debt system and establishing monetary claims on property was the major lever that led to privatizing the land.* As needy plot-holders came to pledge and forfeit their customary property rights as collateral for debt, personal debt became an irreversible lever transferring the customary communal rights enjoyed by the Many (the right to self-support on the land) into private property for a narrowing Few. This financial dynamic brought anarchy and disorder, until the idea of order itself was redefined and indeed, inverted from the traditional system.

The idea of "freedom" underlying Clean Slates
Outright "free" landownership, in the sense of cultivators being able to alienate their lands free of communal restrictions, was slow to come into being. Bronze Age Mesopotamia's idea of freedom was not one of free markets, but of protecting the rural community from the adverse effects of wealth and economic polarization. Instead of the idea of order being one of freedom for creditors to foreclose irreversibly on the lands and bond-pledges of the economically weak, it was one of rulers restoring economic order by annulling personal debts and reversing debtor forfeitures of family members and property. This restored the means of self-support on the land

for the population at large.

In practice this concept of social order and liberty meant that the land — and hence the economic freedom to be self-sufficient — was inalienable, much as America's Bill of Rights holds up certain personal freedoms as being inalienable. Families could not sell their lands under duress without recourse, nor could they forfeit them permanently to creditors. As a result, the earliest inroads of private absentee landlordship were only temporary, save to heads of state (beginning with members of Sargon's family).

The idea of property

The Middle Bronze Age — the half-millennium from 2100 to 1600 BC — is one of the most important transition periods in the history of civilization, precisely because it was a time of decentralization and breakdown. In such periods forward momentum is lost, creating a power vacuum which affords a flexible environment for new structures to emerge.

What gave this half-millennium its quality of "middleness" was the dissolving of centralized public ownership and direction of industry, enabling enterprise to become increasingly private in character. Civilization's first "stock market" developed for shares in the revenue generated by temple properties. The rights to crop revenues on earmarked lands were inherited and subdivided, bought and sold. A real-estate market developed for townhouses, and also for farmland.

Yet there are no Bronze Age words for property as such. The French legal cuneiformist, Emile Szlechter (1958:121), finds that although there are terms and regulations for deposit, pledge, pawn and so forth, "One will look in vain in the Babylonian sources for a general orderly definition of the notion of property. . . . although the expressions *lugal* (in Sumerian) and *belum* (in Akkadian) are habitually translated as *proprietor*, one does not find in the Sumerian and Akkadian vocabulary a term which designates 'property' in the abstract sense of *law of property*." The closest the Middle Bronze Age came to using a term for property was what cuneiformists translate as "domain of the lord," indicating temples as the first permanent absentee owners.

Land tenure thus had not yet evolved into fully autonomous ownership as the modern world knows it. For one thing, Bronze Age land had too many public-service obligations attached to it to be deemed "private" in the

modern sense of the term. It also lacked one of the most important hallmarks
of private property: the ability to be sold freely or otherwise transferred
outside of its local kinship grouping. "Without doubt," concludes Szlechter
(*ibid.*:135f.), "it is not merely a matter of chance or poverty of the Sumerian
and Akkadian languages that has left us no term for property in the actual
sense of the word. It really appears that this notion has not entirely
disengaged itself to the degree found in Roman or modern law."

Military acquisition of land by palace rulers and warlords for their private family use

Temple officials of the old order had been losing ground to the palace and
its nominees at least since the 25th century BC. Circa 2360, the ruler
Lugalanda is found in control of the major Lagash temples, as was his
successor, the reformer Uruinimgina. A generation later the conqueror
Sargon of Akkad placed members of his family (female as well as male) in
key priesthood positions throughout southern Mesopotamia. His successors
purchased large tracts of hitherto group-held land (Gelb, Steinkeller and
Whiting 1991:16f., 26). Subsequent rulers continued this practice.

Meanwhile, new sources of revenue developed in the wake of bureaucratic
decentralization, leaving authority — and in time, land and even temple
workshops — in the hands of local administrators, chieftains and big-men.
In a word, temple offices were privatized.

With regard to the Inanna temple at Nippur during this period, Richard
Zettler (1992: 441, 461) makes the point that "the family archive of the
chief administrator is mixed in with records of the temple operations." In
a similar vein Stone (1987:17f.) finds that business was conducted
increasingly in the private apartments of temple administrators, and adds
that "a few offices had associated prebend fields," but the best estimate of
their value "is that they entitled the owner to a share of the sacrifice." By
the Isin-Larsa period (2000-1800 BC) these revenue flows "had become a
kind of private property which could have been passed on to the heirs of the
owner."

Temple offices and their revenues were being organized along the lines
that modern economists would call profit centers. Each produced an
earmarked usufruct. As this revenue was bequeathed to family members,
it came to be subdivided into smaller and smaller units. The earliest

contracts with regard to temple offices "record the control of whole or half offices," notes Stone (1987:21), "suggesting that these offices had either only been in the family for a short period of time or that they were neither heritable nor divisible before the time of the first contracts." Her hypothesis is that "the offices became heritable and divisible at the time they were given to these families," whose possession of substantial agricultural land suggests a rural foundation.

As background for how this state of affairs may have come about, Stone (1987:72ff., 124) observes that the *Lamentation over the Destruction of Nippur* describes how, during the reign of Ishme-Dagan (1953-1935 BC), "active warfare penetrated the city itself." The city was attacked, most likely by Amorite tribesmen who had entered from the northwestern Arabian-Syrian desert. Their first incursions into Mesopotamia are cited during the reign of Shu-Sin (2037-2029), who built a long fortified wall (the "Martu" or Western wall) to keep them out, but which the Amorites breached in large numbers in 2022.

What may have stopped the fighting, Stone suggests, was the decision by palace rulers to buy off "the leaders of these rural, tribal groups. . . . To stem future rebellion, the king moved them into the city, provided them with a large area of urban real estate, and co-opted the leaders with gifts of real estate and temple offices." Probably Iddin-Dagan (1974-54) and his Isin successors "initiated a program designed to pacify the countryside. Like the British during the mandate period, they brought the tribal leaders into the cities where they could be controlled." The chieftains were given temple positions, or at least the prebend revenues traditionally attached to these positions.

One result was to divorce temple revenue flows from the actual performance of temple functions. Indeed, it would have been a travesty if each individual receiving temple income actually had tried to carry out the associated position for just a few days. Whereas there was only a single *ugula-e* (head administrator) receiving income from the Inanna temple in the Ur III period, "by Old Babylonian times, when up to one hundred may have shared a single office, the ownership of an office can have had little to do with the bureaucratic activities implied by the title," for these titles remained indivisible. There was only one responsible functionary in any given period. Administrative functions thus became separated from the prebend income earmarked to support temple officials. (On this point see also Charpin 1986:62.) Ownership was divorced from management — precisely what Adolph Berle and Gardner Means described in the 1930s as representing the "new capitalism" of our modern epoch!

What was happening was that land, or at least the income associated with it, was passing out of the hands of public institutions to effectively private holders. Based on a study of the clergy of Ur in Hammurapi's dynasty, Charpin (1986:260ff.) likewise concludes that the subdivision of temple prebend incomes must have begun late in the Ur III period. Charpin finds that after 180 to 200 years so many successive bequeathings and partitions of these prebends had occurred that some holders received only a few days' income per year. Typical revenue subdivisions appearing in the cuneiform records are 15 days (1/24th of the 360-day administrative Mesopotamian year), 7° days (1/48th), 5 days (1/72nd), 3 days, and just 1 day per year. "The result, after a century and a half of successive divisions, is an extreme parcellisation of prebends: When we see an individual owning five days of service a year in the Nanna temple, we may conclude that this theoretically signifies that the income is divided among 71 other persons for that year." (The number depends on how many heirs were left by successive generations of each branch of the original family.) The result was an economic organization of temples "as a kind of joint-stock company whose shares have passed into the hands of the town notables." By the first millennium BC this became standard practice throughout the Near East.

Ownership of temple usufruct flows came to be sold with increasing liquidity. Stone (1987:18, 25) finds that after about 1800 BC, temple offices "carried none of the alienation restrictions which applied to the more traditional kinds of property, *i.e.*, fields and houses," for unlike the case with rural subsistence fields, the sale of temple offices was not restricted to one's kinsmen. A new economic class thus came into being: a *rentier* class of temple prebend-holders, history's earliest attested sinecures and absentee owners.

Land transfers occurred through creditor foreclosure
It was largely through debt foreclosure that communal subsistence landholdings were privatized, passing into the hands of public collectors and merchants when cultivators ran into problems. These alienations

occurred especially in times of flood or drought, pestilence and, above all, war, when men were called away from the land to fight or when fighting devastated their own land. Most cultivators had little to pledge as collateral except for their family members - their wives, daughters, sons or servants. As an alternative, cultivators looked for something else that could be pledged. The most desirable asset was land.

What creditors really wanted, of course, was the land's usufruct, which they took as interest. Cultivators continued to work the lands that had been foreclosed. Without their labor, the land rights would not have been very valuable to creditors, for in the early centuries of land mortgaging there was not yet a body of "free" (that is, disenfranchised) seasonal labor for hire.

Pledging the land (or more accurately, its usufruct) as collateral for debt led to absentee ownership and, ultimately, to monopolization of the land, turning it into large estates. By the close of classical antiquity this dynamic culminated in the Roman *latifundia*, on which land-use was shifted to grow export cash crops such as olive oil and wine rather than food to support domestic cultivators. Society polarized between rich and poor, creditors and debtors, landowners and tenants. The wealthiest classes managed to avoid taxes altogether, throwing the fiscal burden onto the lower orders of the population. This destroyed the archaic economic and fiscal balance.

Wealthy landowners gained immunity from taxation
When land passed out of the hands of the community into those of outside appropriators, the economy as a whole suffered. One of the first objectives of these rich and powerful individuals was to avoid paying taxes and related obligations. As they gained exemption from the traditional obligation to use their wealth to support the palace and other communal organs, the fiscal burden was thrown onto the community's poorer and less influential members - a trend that has remained characteristic throughout history. Being outsiders, absentee owners shed the communal duties that were part and parcel of archaic communal landholding - military obligations, *corvée* duties, payment of fees and the customary forms of mutual aid. This left a shortfall that had to be made up by the rural population at large.

The palace for its part lost militarily, for outsiders were not subject to local military service. Indeed, their foreclosures removed the debtor's draft status, preventing communities from fielding their own armed force.

Most Babylonian debts were due in the barley-harvesting month, Simann - the third month of the year, corresponding to our own late May and early June. Just prior to the harvest, cultivators found their resources to be at their lowest ebb. Matters were especially serious if a drought or other natural disaster gave creditors reason to believe that debts were about to be cancelled, and tried to anticipate matters by extorting what they could. To prevent creditors from prematurely trying to collect their debts by coercing debtors to pay and then refusing to refund their money when *misharum* was proclaimed, the Edict of Ammisaduqa (§5) prescribed the death penalty: if a creditor "prematurely collected by means of pressure, he must refund all that he received through such collection or be put to death."

As credit became more privatized, merchant-collectors and other lenders sought to make their financial claims immune from these royal restorations of economic order. Indeed, this seems to have become a major objective of aristocratic or oligarchic opposition to royal authority (especially in Rome, if written tradition is to be relied upon). Rulers for their part overrode such attempts, and in the early centuries they emerged victorious. One finds wealthy landowning creditor families emerging in most major towns, only to disappear suddenly from the cuneiform record.

Clean Slate Proclamations
The severe fiscal problems caused by absentee ownership gave rulers good reason to reinforce the traditional barriers to the land's alienability, and specifically to prevent its transfer to wealthy appropriators. This was particularly the case when the new owners were local officials or chieftains assembling power bases of their own. §37 of Hammurapi's laws annulled any sale of rural fields, orchards or houses that belonged to soldiers, commissaries or feudatories. §38 prohibited these soldiers, commissaries and feudatory tenants from pledging their fief-fields, orchards and houses as collateral for any obligation, or deeding them to their wives or daughters. However, §39 permitted property that already had been bought for cash to be resold, pledged for debt or deeded, evidently on the ground that such market property had passed out of the traditional communalistic or public sphere.

These restrictions against alienating the land were part of a long-standing Mesopotamian tradition. Szlechter (1958:133) points out that although pre-Sargonic records attest to land sales, "when the lease-fields become 'private property' they refer only to houses, orchards or fields, whose area is relatively small." The sellers were professional bodies, and the buyer invariably was the palace (Diakonoff 1982:8-19, 36ff., 67ff.). This is not at all the same thing as property being freely and autonomously transferred among individuals acting on their own account, following the dictates of market forces alone.

The most important royal proclamations deterring absentee landlords from evolving into a permanent wealthy aristocracy upheld the idea that the sale or forfeiture of such lands was only temporary, until the next *misharum* act restored the *status quo ante*. It seems that when rulers enacted *misharum*, all tax and debt tablets were supposed to be handed over to the authorities to be broken, along with all land-property contracts. "Astounding as it must appear to our normally skeptical eyes," concludes Finkelstein (1965:244ff.), instead of the *misharum* institution being "a pious but futile gesture," the fact is that "at the promulgation of the *misharum* formal commissions were established to review real-estate sales."

Finkelstein (1969:58) comments on Ammisaduqa's edict and its predecessors that "the provisions of these acts anticipated a certain amount of skullduggery and fraud aimed at circumventing the effect of the edict." One creditor, for instance, tried to collect the amount nominally due on a debt tablet predating one of Hammurapi's four *misharum* acts. The debtor sued and won on the ground that *misharum* had been declared since the document was drawn up. The judges in this case symbolically broke a clod of earth *in lieu* of the tablet, so that the latter should be considered null and void if the creditor ever again tried to collect.

Another way in which creditors sought to evade the royal proclamations was simply to get debtors to waive their rights following a Clean Slate. A Mari text dated to the sixth year of one of Hammurapi's contemporaries, Zimri-Lim, stipulates that "if an *uddurarum* is instituted, this silver will not be subject to that measure" (ARM VIII 33, discussed by Lemche 1979:17, and Charpin 1987:39). By writing this clause the creditor got his debtor to renounce formally any benefit of the debt remission.

Julius Lewy (1958:24f.) cites similar contractual clauses from another upstream town, Hana, during the reign of Kashtiliashu in the late 1700s. One clause contains "a brief reference to an oath pledging the contracting parties not to contest the validity of their agreement by raising claims against each other." If the complaining party seeks to recover his land, his head is to be "smeared with hot asphalt." Inasmuch as Kashtiliashu's date formulae indicates that he "established (social) justice" at least twice, Lewy infers that it was considered necessary to insert this clause into the contract because "without such a statement, the landed property ... might have been liable to reversion to its former owner." Such clauses are banned in Ammisaduqa's edict of 1646, but are echoed finally in Rabbi Hillel's *prosbul* clause formulated nearly two thousand years later to circumvent the biblical Jubilee Year debt cancellations called for in Leviticus 25.

Anticipating that some creditors might try to perpetrate such deceptions by having their claims "drawn up as a sale or a bailment and then persist in taking interest" (§6), Ammisaduqa's edict voided such documents, thereby annulling the transfers. Creditors who attempted to "sue against the house of an Akkadian or an Amorite for whatever he had loaned him" were threatened with the death penalty, as in §5. (This was just the opposite of subsequent Roman law, which threatened only debtors with death, never creditors!) §7 laid down a similar punishment against creditors who claimed they had not given barley or silver as an interest-bearing loan, but rather as an advance for purchases or equity investment for mutual profit, or some similar form of credit exempted from debt cancellation in §8.

These Clean Slates restored liberty to bond-servants (while returning to their former owners house-born servants who had been pledged to creditors). Thus, not only was the land restored to its traditional equilibrium; so were family structures. But just as land tenure was undercut by the rural usury process, so were the customary family lineage structures.

The "fictive adoption" loophole

Prior to being able to mortgage their land rights, all that poor cultivators had to pledge was their family members. They became bond-servants to the creditors until the debt could be repaid. Inasmuch as interest rates typically mounted up at 33 % per year by 2100 BC, rural debtors often were unable to redeem these pledges. So disruptive was this loss of family members that the laws of Hammurapi dictated that bond-servants should be freed after three years, probably on the logic that creditors got their capital back in this time. Gradually, sanctions against pledging the land for a longer period of time were loosened, beginning with the "fictive adoptions" found in Babylonia by the 18th century BC and spreading upstream along the Euphrates to Nuzi by the 16th century.

It has become an axiom of history that wealthy individuals (usually creditors) tend to appropriate land by stratagems that public policy and laws have not anticipated. Under traditional Mesopotamian land-tenure arrangements, land could not be sold or pledged as collateral for debts, but could only be bequeathed to the heirs of its customary holders. Middle Bronze Age creditors thus could not purchase it directly or get it pledged as collateral for loans on more than a temporary basis. Their solution was to take a strategic detour, arranging to inherit the land upon the death of its seller/debtor, by being "adopted" as his legal son and heir. This ploy became one of history's first documented legal loopholes, opening the gates for major inroads to be made against the principle of self-sufficiency for landed kin-groupings.

The genius of this loophole was that it appeared to reconcile their radical objectives with the conservative force of communal traditions, with the compliance of debtors who were driven to the wall by economic need. In exchange for money to get by, debtors adopted their creditors as sons. Sometimes this entailed having one's daughter marry the creditor or his son. It probably was from such marriage and adoption arrangements that the Babylonian proverb arose, "A creditor has many relatives." When the debtor-landholder died, his adopted creditor-son inherited the land, to the exclusion of the natural sons.

Fighting over the inheritance loophole became a major focal point for legal wrangling over the transfer of property, most notoriously in Nuzi ca. 1500-1600 BC, but apparently already in the Old Babylonian period, according to Stone (1987:24). Describing the practice of "fictive" adoptions, she explains how an indebted Babylonian cultivator would adopt a rich creditor from outside his family, perhaps even from outside his community. The usual ploy was for the creditor (who might well be older than his debtor-adopter) to "pay off his adoptive father's debts and in exchange would inherit the property." The underlying reality, of course, was that the creditor ("son") adopted the debtor as "father" to get his family land-rights. It took some centuries for this process to be abbreviated so that lands could be alienated without the creditor-buyer having to go through the charade of being adopted by the debtor-seller.

In time this charade was dropped altogether, although Szlechter finds in the Old Babylonian period "no case of land appropriation by a family who retains possession and whose proprietor can dispose of it while living." This epoch thus was still far from developing the idea of private property rights in rural land. When such exclusive rights came into being, it was essentially in a negative way, in that it represented a loss of cultivation rights by the population at large, and also a loss to the palace.

In her subsequent study of *Adoption in Old Babylonian Nippur* (1991:2f.), Stone elaborates how Babylonia's "shallow patrilineal lineages" succumbed to the spread of inheritance contracts in which "the adoptee takes on the social role of the son or daughter," standing to receive land rights through inheritance "while the adopter [that is, the debtor] may receive an adoption payment [the *de facto* loan]. . . . the text may describe the monthly and annual rations which are to be delivered by the adoptee to support his new father until his death," these payments representing compensation for granting the land's use-rights as a legacy. The witnesses to such contracts are listed, and "the penalties for breaking the contract are spelled out."

One such contract finds a debt-ridden cultivator, Ur-Lumma, unable to support himself, yet "prevented by contemporary alienation restrictions from converting his property into cash through sale." He solved the problem by adopting the well-to-do Lu-Bau, son of a prominent temple official, "as his heir in exchange for support. The text includes an oath in which Ur-Lumma and his heirs foreswear all claims to Lu-Bau's new inheritance." For Ur-Lumma, the only way to alienate his property rights to land-use and its usufruct to obtain cash and security in his old age was through the back door of adoption; for Lu-Bau, the only way to obtain good property was through this same route (Stone 1991:9f.). As matters turned out, Lu-Bau died without issue. The natural sons of Ur-Lumma pressed their traditional claims to inherit the property and, "thanks to the accident of Lu-Bau's childlessness, they regained control."

The effect was to concentrate land in the hands of an emerging oligarchy, at the expense of poorer lineages. Such arrangements signal the breakup of family-lineage equality of opportunity. Indeed, creditor values historically have been counterposed to traditional family values; or rather, credit relations become the new basis for kinship arrangements.

The emergence of a landed aristocracy

Hammurapi's feudal-type arrangements were a landmark catalyzing the privatization and secularization of Babylonia's economy. To pursue his ambitious plans of conquest, he needed to win the adherence of local chieftains. His strategy was to co-opt them into the royal bureaucracy, at the price of delegating broad authority to them. "Many of these new bureaucrats," finds Yoffee (1979:13), "appear to have come from mid- to upper-level elites of the community who had certain connections to resources embedded in local organizations that the crown wished to mobilize." Thus, whereas centralization of the economic surplus in the public sector had characterized southern Mesopotamia in the third millennium, Hammurapi sponsored its decentralization. This was the essence of his "feudalism," placing authority and, in time, property in the hands of local administrators, chieftains and headmen as the successors of the earlier temple and palace bureaucracies. In a nutshell, hitherto public offices were privatized.

Many Babylonian mortgage holders were public officials, who obtained land by paying the obligations of insolvent cultivators. What they needed to secure permanent rather than merely temporary title was to unseat rulers. This became easier as palace delegated authority to local headmen through quasi-feudal arrangements. Concerned mainly with securing an overall income and source of soldiers, the palace levied obligations on local communities, to be apportioned by their headmen. By classical antiquity these individuals gained enough power to block rulers from cancelling debts and redistributing the lands. The classical aristocracies overthrew kings altogether, replacing them with senates of elders.

Feudalization of imperial authority blurred the distinction between public and private. Rulers leased public land to well-placed individuals in the royal bureaucracy, and let local chieftains administer their territories on the condition that they turn over a specified yield (proto-taxes and contributions) to support the palace and its armed forces.

The idea was to make this decentralized enterprise yield as much to the palace as public enterprise would have done. This autonomy was part of the *quid pro quo* for getting chieftains and headmen to acquiesce in the palace's empire-building, allowing local head-men broad leeway as long as they provided the palace with the same flow of economic usufructs that would have obtained through its own direct management. Well-placed families thus served in effect as public proxies.

Economic polarization inevitably followed from the dynamics of extending local systems to imperial region-wide ones, going hand in hand with a "feudalization" of authority. The basic economic tension in Babylonia stemmed from the fact that although most creditors were *tamkaru* serving in the royal bureaucracy - and, as such, charged with acting in the public interest - they tended to put their own interests above that of the palace, taking the land's usufruct that formerly was available for taxes as payment for their own extensions of credit. Turning crops over to creditors prevented them from being turned over as royal sharecropping rent or sold to the palace.

This was what Hammurapi's laws sought to restrict, forbidding *tamkaru* from taking land from the families of soldiers. Rulers periodically restored the land's *status quo ante* by annulling all claims denominated in barley, that is, personal debts owed by cultivators, including claims for payment by "ale-women" and other public or quasi-public officials, as distinct from the silver-debts owed by and among merchants.

The designers of this system did not plan for the grey area that developed as rural subsistence landholders pledged and forfeited their land-tenure rights to creditors after falling into debt arrears, at archaic interest rates which were beyond the normal ability to pay in near-subsistence economies.

Rulers took steps to counter this development to the extent that they could do so in the weakening momentum of the Middle Bronze Age. Their delegation of authority did not immediately bring into being an aristocratic ruling class, for as just noted, wealthy families disappear after a few generations. Still, the seeds for such a class were being planted. Palace overrides were being undercut.

Summary
Economic individualism and private property emerged as a result of social devolution, not as deliberately thought out progressive policy
With the environmental breakdown and folk-wanderings during Western civilization's first Dark Age, 1200-750 BC, a new, decentralized mode of social organization emerged. In place of the Bronze Age palaces and

chiefdoms, warlord bands subjugated local populations. In some areas of Greece, for instance, local Mycenaean palace or temple *basilius* administrators simply kept control in their own personal hands. The protective checks of Bronze Age public oversight of wealth were removed as aristocracies unseated rulers at the outset of classical antiquity. Privatization of debt, landownership and workshops destroyed the traditional social balance in which families were assured the means of self-support. With no rulers remaining to cancel rural debts perioically, redistribute the land and free individuals who had fallen into debt bondage, the well-to-do became predators on the weak and poor.

Gradually, sanctions against pledging the land were loosened, beginning with the "fictitious adoptions" found in Babylonia by the 18th century BC and spreading upstream along the Euphrates to Nuzi by the 16th century.

II
Classical Antiquity

Periodic restorations of order did not survive the Bronze Age outside of the Near East and Egypt. Instead of creating corporately autonomous public sectors, Greece and Rome concentrated the focus of enterprise, land-rent, and interest-bearing debt in the households of local chieftains. No palace or temple authority existed in the classical Aegean and Italy to be undercut, for only southern Mesopotamia had created the strong centralized public-sector traditions that gradually diffused throughout the Near East. The Mycenaean palaces were a hybrid "mixed" form, and in any case did not survive after 1200 BC. Where local chieftain-kings emerged in the Dark Age convulsions of 1200-750 BC in Greece and southern Italy, they ended up being unseated by landed aristocracies, much as England's aristocracy curtailed royal power from the 13th century AD onward. For better or worse, these aristocracies replaced central power with their own economic control, leaving no central authority to restore economic balance and order once it was disturbed by the dynamics of debt and growing oligarchic power.

The widening polarization between rich and poor was expressed most characteristically in the conflict between creditors and debtors, ending up as a polarization between large landowners and expropriated dependents and slaves. The biblical examples denounced by Isaiah 5:8-9 reflect a polarization that became most pronounced in Rome. Italy in fact was the westernmost peripheral area of the early first millennium BC that still was a viable part of the Levantine system. (Documents from Spain, Carthage and other Phoenician colonies do not appear in the historical record until these regions are conquered by Rome). Being peripheral, Rome never created the checks and balances that preserved self-sufficiency in Mesopotamia and the Levant.

In place of Clean Slates we find irreversible debt servitude. No economic order proclamations cancelling debts have been found, or time-limits to debt bondage or the forfeiture of property to foreclosing creditors and other wealthy buyers. The result was that Rome became the most extreme and unmitigated oligarchy known in antiquity.

Popular tyrants use the debt and land crisis to take power in 7th-century Greece

The classical Greek and Roman states became closed hereditary bodies, in contrast to more open communities such as medieval Ireland, or Rome at its inception. Largely responsible for closing off access to citizenry was the phenomenon of victorious warlords heading bands of followers who subjugated indigenous peoples and monopolized the land for themselves. Classical citizenship, along with military and social ranking, was defined by one's landholding qualification. (Solon's laws spell out how this was done in Athens.).

In the centuries leading up to the classical age, warlord bands parcelled out Greek lands among their own ranks, initially on a more or less egalitarian basis. But by the 7th century BC, land was becoming concentrated in the hands of wealthy aristocratic families. This phenomenon appears to be linked to the spread of interest-bearing debt from the Levant, via Phoenician and Syrian traders, but the details are unrecorded. What is known is that in Corinth, Cypselus seized power in 657, exiled the city's ruling Bacchiads, redistributed their lands and cancelled rural debts. His successors held power until 580. Much the same happened in Sicyon under Cleisthenes, and also in Megara and other cities in which have-nots mobilized behind popular "tyrants" to expel the leading aristocrats, redistribute their lands and cancel the debt-claims they had built up.

Only in the face of military siege were the wealthy classes inspired to share their land with the citizenry at large and to cancel debts across the board. The objective by this time no longer was to maintain social solidarity, but simply to preempt debtors (whose ranks soon came to include the entire local citizenry) from defecting to invaders who promised general debt cancellation and land redistribution.

Military, class and financial warfare thus became inextricably interwoven as armed conflict took place against the backdrop of an ongoing war between rich and poor, oligarchy and *demos*. By 357 BC Áeneas Tacticus, in his book on warfare, defense and fortification, directed "more than half his military admonitions ... towards preventing treachery and forestalling revolution. The men for whom he wrote his manual were clearly in constant danger of the enemy within their own gates, a peril which became more rather than less acute when armed foes without were threatening the very existence of the state" (Oldfather in Tacticus 1923:17). In Tacticus' own words (XIV):

> ... it is of primary importance to win over the mass of the citizens to a spirit of loyalty, both by other influences and in the case of debtors by the reduction or complete cancellation of interest, and, in cases of especial danger, of some part of the principal, or even all of it when necessary; for such men as these are the most formidable adversaries. Adequate provision must also be made for those who are in want of the necessities of life.

Egypt's debt reform under Bocchoris

The pharaoh Bakenranef, whose name was Grecianized to Bocchoris, ruled Egypt ca. 720-715 BC as one of the two rulers of the short-lived XXIVth "Saite" dynasty. He was the last to govern an independent Egypt, for in 715 Ethiopia invaded and installed Kushite kings, inaugurating the Late Period of foreign rule. It was in the midst of this military crisis that Bocchoris abolished debt-servitude. In conjunction with this act he announced a legal reform requiring all contracts, if they were to be deemed legally binding, to be written rather than oral.

Bocchoris's insistence on written contracts had long been standard Mesopotamian practice. It is attested over a thousand years earlier in the laws of Hammurapi. Egypt's adoption of this reform seems to have been inspired by the recognition that Egyptian creditors, like those elsewhere, were prone to claim what was not rightfully theirs. Under Bocchoris's reform, if a debtor contested the claim of his creditor, the debt was nullified unless the creditor could back up his claim by producing a written agreement, properly executed. Many debts were annulled, on the reasoning that greedy creditors unilaterally had demanded debt balances without justification. As our source, Diodorus of Sicily, summarizes the upshot, "men who had borrowed money without signing a bond, if they denied the indebtedness, might take an oath to that effect and be cleared of the obligation."

This insistence on written contracts seems to have remained in force into Ptolemaic times. Contracts documenting personal obligations were necessary in view of the tendency for creditors to exaggerate the balances due. Indeed, from the Old Babylonian period onward, the protection of debtors by insistence on proper documentation explains why archaeologists find debt records so conspicuous in their excavations.

Bocchoris's reform stopped a serious abuse of the debt process by creditors, but it did not tackle the debt problem directly, as had the Clean Slates of Mesopotamia and Solon's *seithachtheia* in Athens. Generically, it was a legal reform and only incidentally a Clean Slate. There is no indication of a land redistribution, reflecting the degree to which Egypt's land tenure had diverged from that of the rest of the Mediterranean region by the 7th century BC.

Rulers found it desirable and practical to cancel personal debts

Modern suspicions that archaic debt cancellations were radical acts or "reforms" are controverted by a simple fact. It was relatively easy for Mesopotamian and Egyptian rulers to cancel personal debts and free debtors who had been reduced to bondage *because most such debts were owed to the public sector* - the palace or temples, or to their collectors, *e.g.* the *tamkaru* merchants in southern Babylonia. Thus, rulers cancelled debts owed ultimately to themselves.

The logic underlying royal Clean Slates was never spelled out, but the Roman historian Diodorus (I.79), writing ca. 40-30 BC, got to the heart of matters when he explained why the pharaoh Bocchoris abolished debt-servitude and cancelled undocumented debts, by ruling "that the repayment of loans could be exacted only from a man's estate, and under no condition did he allow the debtor's person to be subject to seizure." The social context for this edict was the growing military threat from Ethiopia. According to Diodorus, Bocchoris's rationale was that "the bodies of citizens should belong to the state, to the end that it might avail itself of the services which its citizens owed it, in times of both war and peace. For he felt that it would be absurd for a soldier, perhaps at the moment when he was setting forth to fight for his fatherland, to be haled to prison by his creditor for an unpaid loan, and that the greed of private citizens should in this way endanger the safety of all."

This is much how Bronze Age rulers must have reasoned. Hammurapi's laws blocked creditors from taking for themselves the usufruct of tenants on royal and other public lands, and on communal lands that owed manpower and military service to the palace. Creditor attempts to take such lands for themselves threatened to strip the rural sector of its ability to fill the military draft, in an age when warfare was endemic and mercenary armies still lay largely in the future. Such privatization of hitherto communal or royal land thus threatened to bring about fiscal, economic and military disorder in the subsistence rural economies of the Middle and Late Bronze Age. Palace rulers had not yet become economic predators of the land; that would come only with the first-millennium flourescence, and formed the crux of Israelite opposition to such rulers.

Solon frees the land

Matters were moving toward a similar crisis in Athens in 594, when the city's leaders turned over emergency powers to Solon as *archon* ("premier"). He freed the land from debt claims, freed Athenians who had been reduced to debt servitude (and even sold abroad as slaves), and permanently banned debt-servitude for Athenian citizens. Athens also prohibited alien ownership of the land, thereby preventing foreign creditors from lending money against land as collateral and then foreclosing. (Most bankers were foreigners in the 6th and 5th centuries BC.) However, citizenship could be lost through debt to domestic creditors foreclosing on the land.

As safeguards to widespread access to the land were dismantled, the guarantee of economic freedom became more tenuous. The growing power of absentee landholders narrowed the citizen body. Landholding became more concentrated, shrinking the ability of societies to field their own peasant-infantry. This was antiquity's Grand Dynamic or, as Marxists like to say, internal contradiction.

Solon was followed by the popular tyrant Peisistratus and his sons, and in 411 by Cleisthenes, who organized the Athenian democracy by dividing the land and population symmetrically into local demes. Public obligations were standardized, and were owed by the local units collectively, with headmen appointed by lot to apportion public obligations. The guiding political philosophy was one of standardization and regularity.

Sparta's Lycurgan reforms are emulated by Agis and Cleomenes

Sparta's "Lycurgan" reforms ca. 700 BC established a citizen-army of "equals" (*homoioi*), although its "Dorian" settlers turned the indigenous occupants into public serfs, called helots. (The term "serfs" is anachronistic. Their status was deteriorating toward slavery, see Oliva 1971:39-44.) The reforms represent the earliest Greek reaction to the economic polarization stemming from the spread of trade, money and the introduction of debt during 750-700 BC. Sparta's political reaction aimed to establish an underlying standardization among its citizens, suppressing all social distinctions by banning precious metal money and conspicuous consumption (including excessive funerary spending). The Spartans were to take their meals in common (the *syssitia*), and to use their time practicing military tactics. As for the helots, they were not owned by private individuals, but were communally assigned, along with the land they worked. (Toynbee 1969 remains the classic discussion of the Lycurgan reforms. For the Spartan economic evidence as a whole, see Fuks 1984.)

The hoped-for equilibrium was destroyed by Sparta's military success in the Peloponnesian War against Athens and its allies (431-404 BC). Victory drew in riches, filling the land with monetary gold and silver, and enabling an oligarchy to emerge. It seems that toward the end of the war or shortly thereafter the "Law of Epitadeus" permitted *kleros* subsistence lands to be alienated in ways other than through inheritance. In fact, wealthy Spartans hit upon a similar legal loophole to that which had been developed over a millennium earlier in Babylonia and Nuzi: testation of the land to wealthy buyer-creditors. In Sparta's case it was not necessary for the seller-debtor to go to the extreme of adopting his creditor. He could bequeath his estate simply in exchange for a money-gift, or for any other reason.

Plutarch's source, the third-century Stoic Phylarchus, invents a melodramatic explanation in typically Stoic fashion, distracting attention from the more prevalent financial motivation at work. A father, spitefully wishing to disinherit an ungrateful son, established a fateful precedent which subsequently enabled impoverished family heads to bequeath their lands to creditors or other outside buyers.

The result was that Sparta's upper aristocracy (its *ephor* families and the two royal houses) monopolized most of the land, and held much of the population in debt-bondage. Writing ca. 330, Aristotle (*Politeia* 1270b) saw clearly that Sparta's problems stemmed from a worsening division of its land. Phylarchus and Plutarch likewise pointed to changes in Sparta's land tenure arrangements as the cause of its economic polarization and disenfranchisement of its citizen body. As Fuks (1984:236,238) emphasizes, what did Sparta in was a dearth of citizen-soldiers, not of population as such. There is no hint of ancient writers trying to blame the problems caused by inequitable land distribution on such non-economic causes as "irreplaceable losses in war, of barrenness of Spartan women, of dangers of inbreeding, which bulk large in modern comments." Rather, Plutarch (Modern Library ed.:962f.) describes how the Spartans welcomed the rhetra of Epitadeus "out of greed, made it valid, and so destroyed the most excellent of institutions." Through a combination of direct purchase and usury, "the rich men without scruple drew the state into their own hands, excluding the rightful heirs from their succession; and all the wealth being centered upon the few, the generality were poor and miserable," The impoverished families had to work at occupations unworthy of free men. Class antagonisms intensified, destroying the former patriotism. The spirit of Lycurgus was long gone.

Matters were aggravated by the fourth-century struggle with Persia. Spartan sea power, hitherto financed largely by Persian subsidies, was destroyed in 391 at Cnidus. After losing considerable territory to Philip of Macedon, Sparta was defeated even more severely by Alexander the Great and never recovered. The absence of prosperity worked to concentrate wealth just as the former infusion of wealth had done, even more so inasmuch as families had to borrow to make ends meet (see Tarn 1925:112ff. and Oliva 1971:209ff). By enabling families to alienate their lands, the "freer" market-oriented laws made possible the loss of this property.

By the time Agis IV took the throne in 244 BC, the richest hundred families had dispossessed most of the population. It seems that only about 700 citizens were left on the eve of Agis' proposed rhetra. Of these, "about one hundred were land-rich. The other six hundred were land-poor," barely able to pay their contribution to the common meals. "The rest were landless or so land-poor that they lost their census in consequence of their poverty and became *hypomeiones*" (Fuks, 1984:235). Agis and his successor, Cleomenes III, sought to restore the old way of life by cancelling the debts and, in Cleomenes' case, abolishing the *ephor* class, enfranchising the *perioeci* "dwellers around" Sparta, and freeing the helots. But Agis was killed by the oligarchic faction, Cleomenes was exiled to Egypt, and civil war erupted, giving way to the anti-oligarchic tyrant Nabis.

According to Plutarch (*Agis* 8:1-4), Agis sought to rebuild Sparta's citizen army to a level of 4,500 men. Each would have his own *kleros*, be freed from all debts, and would be trained in the old "Lycurgan" spirit of austere equity. To compensate for the fact that much of Sparta's citizenry had been disenfranchised, many *perioikoi* and *xenoi* ("dwellers around" and foreigners) were incorporated into the expanded 4,500-man army and its 4,500-lot subsistence support land, which was to be equally apportioned among the reformed citizen body.

Agis proposed that "every one should be free from their debts, and that all the lands should be divided in equal portions," the Spartan lands into 4,500 lots and the outlying lands into another 15,000 lots to be shared "among those of the country who were fit for service as heavy-armed soldiers, the first among the natural-born Spartans." Fifteen companies of soldiers were to be formed, "with a diet and discipline agreeable to the laws of Lycurgus." However, this proposal was defeated by a single vote. In the political infighting which followed, Agis nearly succeeded in driving the oligarchic leaders out of the city, but new ephors were elected and cited Agis' supporters Lysander and Mandroclidas "to answer for having, contrary to law, cancelled debts, and designed a new division of lands." Agis and Cleombrotus responded with a bloodless coup (waged partly with men release from prison for the occasion) and set about putting their economic program into practice.

However, relates Plutarch, one heavily indebted landowner persuaded Agis to divide his program into two parts, and first to cancel the debts without redistributing the lands. The result was an object lesson in how *not* to cancel debts. Wealthy landholders were able to get their lands freed of debt, while the landless population found themselves also free of debt but without the promised means of support on the land. The oligarchic leader Leonidas returned from exile and captured Agis. The ephors condemned him to be strangled to death, as were his mother and grandmother - Sparta's first regicides.

Cleomenes III took up the Lycurgan idealism of Agis, and carried through his program of land redistribution, common meals and other egalitarian reforms. But by this time the rest of Greece had succumbed to oligarchies, and viewed Sparta's revolution as a threat to its economic and political stability. The Achaean League invited the Macedonian ruler Antigonus Doson to suppress Sparta, which he invaded in 222, chasing Cleomenes to the court of Ptolemy III in Egypt, where he committed suicide in 220.

Cleomenes' reforms were rapidly undone, but after a civil war the tyrant Nabis crushed the nobility, as tyrants had done throughout Greece in the 7th century BC. As the aristocratic Polybius (XIII.6) describes the upshot, Nabis and his supporters "utterly exterminated those of the royal houses who survived in Sparta, and banishing those citizens who were distinguished for their wealth and illustrious ancestry, gave the property and wives to the chief of his own supporters and to his mercenaries."

Rome was drawn into this Aegean conflict by anti-reformist oligarchic cities of the Achaean League. The upshot is described from quite a different perspective than that of Polybius by Perry Anderson (1974:58), drawing on Livy, XXXIV.33-43 and XXXI.17f:

> This last explosion of Hellenic political vitality is too often tucked away as an aberrant or marginal postscript to classical Greece . . . In one of the most dramatic confrontations of Antiquity, at the exact point of intersection between the eclipse of Greece and the ascent of Rome, Nabis confronted Quinctus Flaminius - commanding the armies sent to stamp out the example of Spartan subversion - with these pregnant words: "Do not demand that Sparta conform to your laws and institutions . . . You select your cavalry and infantry by their property qualifications and desire that the few should excel in wealth and the common people be subject to them. Our law-giver did not want the state to be in the hands of the few, whom you call the Senate, nor that any one class should have supremacy in the State. He believed that by equality of fortune and dignity there would be many to bear arms for their country."

With Rome's intercession the economic flourishing of Greek democracy effectively comes to an end, although a half-century of fighting still remained. As in the time of Tacticus two centuries earlier, both attackers and defenders of cities continued to bid for the loyalties of urban populations by promising debt cancellations. The Achaean League, which first had called upon Rome for help when fighting the Aetolians and Spartans, ended up fighting Rome itself. The former military supporter had becoming a more serious burden than domestic Greek rivals. In the winter of 147/6, Critolaus, general of the Achaean League, sought to mobilize region-wide support against Rome by sending "around magistrates not to exact money from debtors, nor to receive prisoners arrested for debt, and to cause loans on pledge to be held over until the war should be decided. By this kind of appeal to the interests of the vulgar [the aristocratic historian Polybius is speaking], everything he said was received with confidence, and the common people were ready to obey any order he gave" (Polybius, *History*, XXXVIII.9).

But there would be no more land redistributions or debt cancellations until the abortive revolt of Aristonicus in Asia Minor in 133 BC, also put down brutally by Rome as it absorbed Asia as the republican empire's richest province, whose booty funded the emergence of its "knightly" *publicani* class created by Tiberius Gracchus. During the Mithradatic wars in 88 BC, the wealthy city of Ephesus offered its residents a general cancellation of debts in order to counter Mithradates' similar promises.

Such actions suggest that the Stoics and other philosophers formulating doctrines of social equity and debt cancellation did so largely out of enlightened self-interest rather than either pure altruism or a malaise or disdain for their own class interests. They needed to protect their cities from internal strife in the face of ever-present external military conflict. To bring into being an impoverished urban class, especially one of nonfighters, was perceived to be short-sighted and self-defeating. The archaic philosophic ideal of general social balance and equity was carried over into Stoicism, whose adherents were not egalitarian extremists but rather, quite simply, sought to protect their societies against the development of a debt-ridden underclass.

Monopolization of the land in Rome

Matters were not so salutary in Rome. Debt-servitude was practiced from
the outset, but Cicero (*de officiis* 2.78-80) reflected the spirit of his times
in condemning the redistribution of land and cancellation of debts. The
plebeians never were able to break the patricians' stranglehold on the
economy. Matters were especially serious for soldiers called away from the
land to engage in the almost constant fighting that enabled Rome to conquer
central Italy. In effect the peasantry was fighting for its own expropriation.
Their families were forced into debt, and were absorbed (along with their
lands) into the estates of their well-to-do creditors.

A time-honored way to alleviate this problem was to settle war veterans
on new lands, either the territories they had helped conquer or the domestic
ager publicus populi. But Rome's life and death struggle with Carthage
changed matters dramatically. Toward the end of the war, ca. 206 BC, the
senate called upon all families to contribute whatever jewelry or other
precious belongings they could to help the war effort. The gold and silver
was melted down in the temple of Juno Moneta (whence our word "money"
derives) to strike the coins used to hire mercenaries that helped defeat
Carthage. However, after the war was won, the aristocrats demanded that
their contributions be treated as loans. The treasury was bare, and all that
Rome had to offer was its rich public land, above all the Campagna. This
was turned over to the leading war contributors rather than used to settle
returning war veterans. In *Hannibal's Legacy* (1965), Arnold Toynbee
describes this giveaway as representing the classical epoch's single most
detrimental privatization of hitherto public property.

By the first century BC, Rome found itself engulfed in a long Social War
(133-29 BC), fought largely over the debt and land issues. The patricians
won, and used their political power to reduce as much of the population as
possible to debt servitude and outright chattel slavery on the land. Government
became an alliance of the wealthiest families, through their exclusive role
in the senate. By the time Julius Ceasar introduced personal bankruptcy
laws, they were for the rich only, leaving the lower classes untouched.
When tax forgiveness came, emperors proclaimed it only for the rich, not
for the impoverished cultivator-owners.

The wealthiest families managed ultimately to gain immunity from the public obligations which landholders traditionally had owed their communities. Taxes became regressive and the economy polarized between rich and poor, undermining society's fiscal position.

These events form the background for Rostovtzeff's narrative of how enterprise was stifled. The ultimate object of wealth throughout all antiquity was to buy land, for that was the means not only of self-support, but of the ability to support dependents and retainers, commercial earning power and, ultimately, political power. By the imperial period which inaugurated the modern era, there was no thought of restoring equitable property relations or freeing the land from its debt burden. By the time usury and human slavery were banned in the fourth century, it was because the rich had everything. Their objective in banning slavery and usury was simply to stem the depopulation and assure a supply of soldiers to defend what was left of the empire from Germanic incursions from the north. In 396, Constantine removed the imperial seat from Rome to Byzantium - Constantinople, the "Second" or "New" Rome - leaving the western half of the empire to sink into abject insolvency and subsistence production.

There was an unanticipated silver lining to all this. The worse a crisis is, the more far-reaching the economic reforms tend to be. Commercial activity throughout the Roman Empire became so stifled by the end of the fourth century of our era that the greatest Clean Slate in history was proclaimed. Slavery was banned outright, along with usury. Life on the land stabilized, albeit on merely a subsistence level as slaves on Rome's great *latifundia* estates were reorganized to provide serfs with their own cottages.

III
The Byzantine collapse

While the western European half of the Roman Empire fell into poverty after the imperial capital was shifted to Constantinople in 396, the East Roman Byzantine half regained its economic momentum and prosperity by the 7th century. Grounded on the preservation of rural stability, imperial policy sought to avoid a relapse resulting from the corrosive effects of usury. For many centuries royal rulings, called Novels, prohibited mortgaging the land and its attendant monopolization by large landowners, on much the same rationale that had motivated Bronze Age rulers: a military one. Just as Babylonia's army three thousand years earlier had been recruited from the ranks of peasant freeholders, so was the Byzantine army - and so too were the best emperors.

Basil I (867-886), founder of the Macedonian dynasty, was the son of a peasant and had spent most of his life in modest circumstances before ascending quickly - and, surprisingly, unopposed - to reform Byzantium's fiscal and legal systems. He replenished the army's ranks by ordering that the vouchers of insolvent debtors be burned, and his lawbook, the *Epanagoge*, prohibited creditors from taking fields as collateral. To prevent rural instability from recurring, Basil banned agrarian lending at interest, save for the loophole of permitting the money of orphans and other minors to be lent out to provide an income for their support. His laws restricted alienation of the land "by giving the right of first refusal to the other members of the community, either individually or collectively" (Toynbee

70

1973:147). However, his successor Leo VI (886-912) permitted interest of
5°% to be charged, claiming that the ban on rural mortgages burdened the
economy. This and subsequent Novels opened the way for the large
dhynatoi to re-appropriate the land. (Novel 114, for instance, removed the
right of first refusal to local community members.)

What forced a reversal of Leo's "market oriented" philosophy was a
wave of rural credit disasters and famine. The need to raise troops to defend
the empire's eastern front entailed the domestic danger of empowering
landlords and the armies under their command to become an autonomous
force threatening palace rule. After a six-year turmoil following Leo's
death, the imperial crown again passed to a man of lowly origin, Romanus
Lecapenus (919-944). A soldier's son who had distinguished himself by his
strength and bravery, he managed to surround himself with competent
advisors.

Brehier (1977:111) describes Romanus as "the first emperor to take
legislative measures to check the disturbing spread of large estates at the
expense of smaller properties and to preserve the integrity of military
properties, fundamental to the administration of the themes and the
recruitment of an indigenous army." Toynbee (1973:153) paraphrases one
of his novels, probably from the year 929 following Byzantium's victory
on its eastern frontier. Famine had plagued the countryside during the
winter of 927/8, forcing many peasants to mortgage their lands to wealthy
creditors, who absorbed the properties into their own holdings and enserfed
the former freeholders. With the memory of the rural credit disasters under
Leo VI still fresh, the emperor wrote a preamble avowing that: "We have
left nothing undone to liberate districts and villages and cities from the
enemy. . . . Now that we have achieved these magnificent successes in
putting an end to the aggression of the foreign enemy, what about the
domestic enemy in our own household? How can we refrain from dealing
severely with him?" This question might apply just as well to Babylonia
three thousand years earlier.

Romanus' novel of 934 "stigmatized the egoism of the powerful, and
also, without actually ordering the general eviction of all proprietors who
held properties belonging to the poor, annulled all transactions, gifts and
legacies made after 922, and laid it down that any property which had been
acquired for less than half the reasonable price should be handed back

without indemnity. On the other hand, if the purchase had been fair, the property could be redeemed within three years provided the money paid for it was refunded. "The small property" wrote the emperor, "is particularly useful for the payment of taxes and the performance of military service. Everything would be imperilled if it disappeared." Romanus, who was himself the son of a holder of a military property, understood the danger which threatened the free peasantry, which was the best support of the state" (Brehier *loc. cit.*).

Subsequent emperors were not so strong. As creditors monopolized the land, they weakened the fiscal position, and hence the ability to field a Byzantine army. Indeed, as tensions mounted between the emperors and large landholders, Byzantium cut off its nose to spite its face. To prevent warlords emerging from the ranks of the large landowners (as local commanders) and turning their troops against Constantinople itself, the emperors avoided funding the army. In any event, collecting taxes became all but impossible as local autonomy increased. The landowners welcomed this warlord strife, for by countering royal power, it minimized the emperor's ability to collect taxes. (At least there was not yet any public debt! That modern outlet for surplus funds was a western European innovation.)

Constantine Porphyrogenitus (944-959) revived many of Romanus' laws, and sought to make the legal system more accessible to small claimants. After he died (probably by poison in 959), the crown passed to the incompetent Romanus II (959-963), but matters were stabilized by the nearly 50-year rule of Basil II (976-1059), the longest in Byzantine history.

During his early twenties the military and landed aristocracy retained control of the leading palace advisors, seeking above all (as aristocracies invariably do) to prevent the emergence of a strong emperor. However, as two warlords, Bardas Sclerus and Bardas Phocas, vied for control of the empire during the early 980s, the young emperor came to realize that to survive in control of matters, he must enter a life and death fight against the landlords. This he achieved by rescuing the still-free peasantry from being reduced to serfdom and hence clientship to the large landholders. To reverse the wholesale forfeiture of lands that had taken place, Basil moved on New Year's Day, 996, to abolish the law which prescribed a period of forty years of tenure before ownership of property could be established. Instead, he ruled that all lands which had been acquired since the first law of Romanus Lecapenus in 922 must be restored to their original owners without any indemnity, even those taken over by the Church. The preamble to this novel, regarded as a gloss added by Basil, protests indignantly against the scandal caused by important families such as the Phocae and the Maleini, who had kept unjustly acquired properties in their possession for more than a hundred years.

This law was applied with extreme severity. Philokales, who had usurped a number of large properties and bought himself high palatine offices, was reduced to his original status of simple peasant, and the authorities even went so far as to destroy the buildings he had erected. (Brehier 1977:150)

Basil's "chief weapon against the maintenance of large properties was a reform of the so-called *allelengyon*. This system, whereby local communities were jointly responsible for an annual sum payable to the imperial fisc, was now altered in such a way that the financial burden fell solely on the owners of large estates, the poor being exempted." The leading landed families tried to get the patriarch Sergius to intervene on their behalf, but with little effect.

Basil II resembled Hammurapi not only in his exceptionally long rule, but in the fact that he was obliged to establish a feudal-type system as the price of consolidating imperial power, rewarding supporters who were loyal with tax exemptions. This had the ultimate effect of weakening Byzantium's fiscal condition, while catalyzing a transition to feudalism in the sense of establishing personal loyalties to a ruler who could hand out financial favors or impose heavy burdens at his own personal discretion.

Tax exemption for religious and other institutional landholdings
The problem by no means was limited to large private landowners, but extended to the monasteries and other religious bodies which played an important role in the East Roman Empire (as they also did in the West, of course). For instance, when Byzantine officials descended on the empire's Bulgarian province after the region finally was conquered in 1018, Basil was obliged to "win the peace" by issuing *exkousseia*, "excusances." Their pedigree can be traced back to the Middle Babylonian *kudurru* exempting local towns and temple precincts from royal taxation. Such privileges,

writes Oikonomides (1988:321f.), were distributed to quell the revolt of local potentates, by rewarding "those who remained faithful to the emperor in order to secure their support."

This was the root of feudal privileges: making local leaders - above all the clergy, in this case - dependent on the emperor's will, not *ipso facto* as a result of their belonging to a class of exempted properties. "What used to be a general privilege for all priests, now appears as a special favor granted to the archbishop, and concerns only a limited number of those under his jurisdiction. The privileges of Bari [in Grecian Italy] and Ohrid [in Bulgaria] are identical from that point of view."

Down through the 10th century, emperors had sought "to contain the expansion of big landownership, including ecclesiastical, expecially under Nicephoros Phokas and Basil II in the early years of his reign," by abolishing the traditional ecclesiastical exemption from corvées and *leitourgoi*. This revived Byzantium's fiscal position, at the expense of the clergy and its traditional privileges. However, adds Oikonomides (*op. cit.*:323-5), "the state, instead of abolishing the privilege completely, tried to control it by establishing limited numbers of exempt clerics for each diocese. It thus reserved to itself the right to increase the number when it so wished in order to win the favour of a prelate or of the inhabitants of a region." Bishops, for instance, were allowed to distribute a specified number of exemptions to individuals within their sees. "Consequently, the new approach created automatically a client relationship between the prelates and their subordinates."

Actually, Oikonomides points out: "What appears to us as a major gift, is in fact a limitation of pre-existing privileges," for there was a fundamental shift from the Late Roman situation.

In the Late Roman Empire traditional privileges concerned a whole class of individuals, while the 'gifts' of Basil II reflect all the characteristics of medieval privileges, i.e. exceptional treatment granted by the sovereign to individual cases in anticipation of, if not in exchange for, the favors of the recipient. The difference is essential. Moreover, what was initially, in the Byzantine case, a real limitation of the extent of the privilege, ended up by becoming a loosening by the institution of the tight structure of the monarchic state in favor of the centrifugal forces of the privileged aristocrats, among whom the church formed a part. For in effect, the priestly hierarchy was filled mainly with scions of Byzantium's leading landed families. The Late Roman tax exemptions had been granted to the clergy and other public bodies across the board by virtue of their public roles, *contemplatione dignitatis atque militiae, laborum contemplatione*. As these privileges concerned automatically large numbers of people, their distribution had to be parsimonious, their limits clearly defined and strictly enforced. The medieval privileges, on the contrary, emanating from a personal and exceptional favor could be granted easily for each specific case, without a clear awareness of the possible accumulation of such privileges and their results on the finances of the state. These privileges could easily be considered as hereditary, especially when granted to members of large and powerful families. They were easily granted and in large numbers in moments of political instability, when local magnates - or church representatives, like those who obtained Basil's exemptions - could influence or even bring pressure to bear on the central authority. A procedure therefore that was introduced with the idea of limiting the special privileges of the church, ended up by reinforcing them at the expense of the state.

The benefits of such exemptions were passed on to tenants (*paroikoi*), but at the expense both of other landlords and the palace. By renting from the church, they gained exemption from the royal land tax (*klerikotopion*). "Their exemption from certain fiscal burdens profited mainly the bishop, who received at least part of the exemption and who was thus in a better position to attract to his lands the manpower necessary for their cultivation, by offering prospective lessees more advantageous conditions than those of non-exempt landowners."

Actually, large religious institutions have enjoyed fiscal exemption in nearly all known societies, reflecting their autonomous status on a par with the palace ("the state"). This was far from creating problems in Mesopotamia, for at the inception of the Bronze Age, Sumerians endowed their temple as surplus-creating centers, many centuries prior to the development of taxing the community at large (inasmuch as a substantial private-sector surplus had not yet come into being to tax).

Matters were different in Egypt, where each pharaoh's soul was cared for by a cult incorporated upon his death - an entire funerary territory and population, cutting people and their economic energy out of society's commercial operations to support a public overhead which, in economic terms, was unproductive of any surplus. Via classical antiquity, whose temples became more purely religious institutions rather than commercially productive ones, the transition to feudal times in the Late Middle Ages saw these institutions become productive only in the spiritual world, not that of commerce.

It also is significant that traditional communal inheritance laws were first loosened in medieval times by the Christian Church. In contrast to the practice from Babylonia to Byzantium, rather than poor tenants bequeathing their lands to creditors, wealthy aristocrats gave them to the church for the salvation of their souls. These properties thus passed out of the royal tax domain - until Henry VIII reversed the trend by breaking up England's monasteries in a pre-Thatcherite privatization.

Land monopoly leads to military defeat
By the 11th century the fiscal situation was so weakened that the empire no longer could defend itself. The last stand against the landlords - and enemies at the borders - was made by the Comneni Dynasty founded by Alexius I (1081-1118). However, their position was compromised from the outset. "Since they belonged to the nobility, they abandoned the time-honored offensive of the central government against the great landowners and, to consolidate their dynasty's power, they favored the formation of large apanages and the unlimited increase of monastic properties, thus weakening the authority of the state" (Brehier 1977:202).

To be sure, in the year of his accession, Alexius "seized the goods of numerous noblemen convicted of conspiracy; he made grants or *charisticia* to the profit of individuals from the possessions of monasteries in exchange for the military services of their tenants (*paroikoi*); he tightened up taxation and debased the coinage." But his made him so unpopular that "people in the provinces preferred barbarian to Byzantine rule, and in 1095 the towns of Thrace opened their gates to the Comans" (*ibid.*:207).

Unable to raise taxes to fund a royal army, and indeed, fearful of leaving troops in the hands of commanders drawn almost inherently from the ranks of the upper aristocracy, the Byzantine emperors had few resources to counter the pressures from the Turks gaining control in the eastern Arab states and Normans pressing in from Italy, joining forces with Venice and Genoa with their navies, and German emperors in a tenuous partnership with the papacy while the Crusades set vast troop movements in motion from western Europe across Byzantium to the Holy Land.

In 1204 Byzantium fell before the small army of Crusaders who looted Constantinople on behalf of their Venetian creditors, with whom they had reached a booty-sharing arrangement to finance the naval expedition against Byzantium. Actually, the sacking of Constantinople was an anticlimax, following the economy's erosion in the 11th century when the emperors followed the disastrous policy of reducing the army to prevent the local landowners (who were the army commanders) from using the troops against them. They could not solve the problem of promoting wealth without economic polarization strengthening the nobility in its opposition to any centralized royal overrides to oligarchic wealth-seeking, land monopolization and, ultimately, regicide.

Bibliography

Andelson, Robert V., ed. (1991), *Commons Without Tragedy* (London).

Anderson, Perry (1974), *Passages from Antiquity to Feudalism* (London)

Adams, Robert, (1981), *Heartland of Cities* (Chicago).

Bréhier, Louis (1977), *The Life and Death of Byzantium* (Amsterdam).

Charpin, Dominique (1986), *Le Clerge d'Ur au siecle d'Hammurapi* (Geneva-Paris).

"   (1987), "Les Decrets Royaux a l'Epoque Paleo-babylonienne, a Propos d'un Ouvrage Recent," *AfO* 34:36-44.

Dandamaev, Muhammed (1984), *Slavery in Babylonia, from Napopolassar to Alexander the Great (626-331 BC)* (De Kalb, Ill.)

Diakonoff, Igor (1969), *Ancient Mesopotamia: Socio-Economic History* (Moscow).

"   (1982), "The Structure of Near Eastern Society before the Middle of the 2nd Millennium BC," *Oikumene* 3:7-100.

Finkelstein, Jack J. (1961), "Ammisaduqa's Edict and the Babylonian 'Law Codes," *JCS* 15:91-104.

"   (1965), "Some New *misharum* Material and its Implications," in AS 16 (*Studies in Honor of Benno Landsberger on his Seventy-Fifth Birthday*):233-246.

"   (1969), "The Edict of Ammisaduqa: A New Text," *RA* 63:45-64.

Fuks, Alexander (1984), *Social Conflict in Ancient Greece* (Leiden).

Gelb, Ignace; Steinkeller, Piotr; and Whiting, Robert M. Jr., (1991), *Earliest Land Tenure Systems in the Near East: Ancient Kudurrus* (Chicago = OIP 104).

Guerdan, René (1956), *Byzantium: Its Triumphs and Tragedy* (London [French ed., 1954]).

Hardin, Garrett (1968), The Tragedy of the Commons", *Science* (pp.1243-48).

"   (1991), "The tragedy of the *Unmanaged* Commons . . ." in

Andelson 1991:162-85.

Hudson, Michael (1992), "Did the Phoenicians Introduce the Idea of Interest to Greece and Italy - And If So, When?" in Günter Kopcke and Isabelle Tokumaru, *Greece Between East and West: 10th-8th Centuries BC* (Mainz):128-143.

"   (1993), *The Lost Tradition of Biblical Debt Cancellations* (New York).

"   (1994), *Bronze Age Finance* (in press).

Kraus, Fritz R. (1984), *Königliche Verfügungen in altbabylonischer Zeit* (SD 11, Leiden).

Lemche, Niels Peter (1979), "*Andurarum* and *misharum*: Comments on the Problems of Social Edicts and their Application in the Ancient Near East," *JNES* 38:11-18.

Lewy, Julius (1958), "The Biblical Institution of *Deror* in the Light of Akkaian Documents," *Eretz-Israel* 5.

Oikonomides, N. (1988), "Tax Exemptions for the Secular Clergy under Basil II," Joan Hussey festschr. (Porphyrogenitus):317-26.

Oliva, Pavel (1971), *Sparta and her Social Problems* (Amsterdam and Prague).

Rostovtzeff, Mikhail (1926), *The Social and Economic History of the Roman Empire* (Oxford)

Steinkeller, Piotr (1981), "The Renting of Fields in Early Mesopotamia and the Development of the Concept of 'Interest' in Sumerian," *JESHO* 24.

Stone, Elizabeth (1987), *Nippur Neighborhoods* (Chicago).

"   , and Owen, David I. (1991), *Adoption in Old Babylonian Nippur and the Archive of Mannum-meshu-lissur* (Winona Lake, Indiana).

Szlechter, Emile (1958), "De quelques considérations sur l'origine de la propriété foncière privée dans l'Ancien Droit Mesopotamien," *RIDA*, 3rd ser. 5:121-36.

Tacticus, Aeneas (1923), *On the Defense and Fortification of Positions*, tr. W. A. Oldfather (London and New York).

Tarn, W. W. (1925), *The Hellenistic Age* (Cambridge).

Tawney, R. H. (1912), *The Agrarian Problem in the Sixteenth Century* (London).

Toynbee, Arnold (1965), *Hannibal's Legacy: The Hannibalic War's Effects on Roman Life* (London, 2 vols.).

"   (1969), *Some Problems in Greek History* (London).

"   (1973), *Constantine Porphyrogenitus and his World* (London).

Yoffee, Norman (1977), *The Economic Role of the Crown in the Old Babylonian Period* (Malibu).

"   (1979), "The Decline and Rise of Mesopotamian Civilization: An Ethno-archaeological Perspective on the Evolution of Social Complexity," *American Antiquity*, 44:5-35.

Zettler, Richard (1992), *The Ur III Temple of Inanna at Nippur* (Berlin).

The Health and Wealth of the Nation: A Critique of the Welfare State

G. J. Miller

For more than 150 years Liberal and Socialist reformers have striven to eradicate what they regarded as an unacceptable facet of capitalism; namely the misery and suffering inflected on the poor through indequate nutrition, disease and injury. Largely through their efforts, Britain embarked upon the long journey towards the welfare democracy that it is today. An extra-ordinarily complex system of taxation of wages and of profits (or interest as classical economists call it) has evolved along the way, put together by successive governments to support an expanding social programme aimed at redistribution of wealth to improve the lot of those that capitalism had left relatively deprived. This redistribution has been partly in cash terms and partly in kind in the forms of health care, education and housing. It has come as a considerable shock, therefore, to realise that this effort has largely failed in one of its primary and, what many would claim to be, most important objectives. While as part of the general accumulation of wealth there has been a remarkable improvement in health and life-span through the 20th century, relative inequalities in health between the affluent and the deprived are as entrenched as ever.[1] A very similar situation exists in the USA.[2,3]

1

Social Classes and Their Health in Britain

British society is said to be 'class-ridden': that is, separated into socially cohesive groups divided largely on the basis of occupation. These divisions are re-inforced by ideas of status, or the worth that society attaches to a variety of human attributes - some of them seemingly trivial to an outsider. Class and status are intimately woven, for occupation is one aspect of status and other aspects of the status complex determine opportunities for occupation. Class and status determine power and advantage, and therefore are of fundamental importance for the life-chances of any person in Britain. The rigidity of the class structure of Victorian times is no more, but the realistic social horizons of the lower strata remain relatively limited.

The gap that separates the affluent upper social classes from the poorer lower classes has many dimensions, only one of which is material wealth. Others of fundamental importance are interrelated inequalities in health, life-span, education and environment. The divide between rich and poor is commonly and simplistically thought of in terms of wages, but in Britain most wealth is held in other forms. Thus attempts to quantify relative deprivation on a scale of wages must the crude at best. All studies of wealth are soon bedevilled by disagreements over definition. With life-span, by contrast, there can be no argument. The health dimension of deprivation is quantifiable in ways that the wealth dimension is not, and as such provides a powerful tool with which to assess the effectiveness of interventions meant to alleviate the plight of lower socio-economic groups in society.

The Office of Population Censuses and Surveys (The General Register Office up to 1970) is the guardian of more than 260 million records of births, marriages and deaths - the 'hatches, matches and despatches' as they are called - covering the population of England and Wales since 1837.[4] The records are fully accessible and open to the general public, and the search room of the Office has about 2000 visitors each day. Whereas good records and statistics are collected on disease and mortality, little information accessible to the public is held on land and other forms of wealth, except for limited purposes of taxation. Contrast the workings of the General Register Office with that of H.M. Land Registry established 25 years later in 1862 to register title to land. By 1990, the latter had recorded only 13 million of the estimated 22 million properties in Britain. In many cases, probably the majority, the land values are not known to the Registry; and when they are they may not be revealed. These striking contrasts, openness and completeness for one Register, close secrecy and incompleteness for the other, are remarkable in their apparent inconsistency. Surely a reliable inventory of the nation's land is as important for planning and good government as an inventory of the population that inhabits and depends upon it?

In 1911, Dr T H C Stevenson, statistical superintendent to the Registrar General, Sir Bernard Mallet, introduced a grouping of occupations as recorded on the national Census and death certificates, 'designed to represent as far as possible different social grades'.[5] The timing of this innovation was no accident, as will become apparent. The classification grouped occupations according to the degree of skill involved and the social position implied. Initially there were five groups, with textile workers, miners and agricultural workers held in separate categories because of special interest in their mortality. For the 1921 Census, these three occupations were reallocated to one of the 5 groupings which today are:

I	Professional
II	Intermediate (manager, nurse, teacher etc)
III N	Skilled non-manual (typist, shop assistant, etc)
III M	Skilled manual (miner, driver, etc)
IV	Partly skilled manual (farm worker, etc)
V	Unskilled manual

All users of this system have acknowledged its subjective nature. The occupational structure of each class must change with social attitudes and value judgements. For example, clerks were relegated from social class I to II in 1911 and then to III in 1931. Following the comparative fortunes of the classes over long periods of time is therefore complicated by these drifts in occupations from one to another. Social class V is diminishing in size as occupations drift up to IV. Does therefore a change in the mortality rate of social class V reflect a real deterioration in the health of this stratum of society, or simply a drift in its composition towards a residue of occupations that always have had a particularly poor health record? Those using this system to explore inequalities in health in British society have had to use some ingenuity to overcome the many potential pitfalls.

Death rates in the social classes
By using occupation as recorded on the decennial Censuses, the size of each social class can be measured at the beginning of each decade. Also by examination of the occupation stated on the death certificate, the numbers of deaths can be counted in each social class within a few years of the Census. These summary data permit the calculation of death rates by social class. Before these rates can be reliably compared, however, the findings need to be adjusted for any age differences between the social classes. The usual way of doing this is to calculate the standardised mortality ratio (SMR). By taking the death rates in each age group for England and Wales as a whole (the standard population), we can calculate the number of deaths that would have been expected in each social class had its death rates at each age been those of the standard population (multiply the number in each age group by the standard population's death rate at that age. Do this for each age group and total the numbers of deaths expected). The observed number of deaths in that social class is then expressed as a percentage of the expected number. When the SMR is below 100 or above 100, the mortality experience of that social class is respectively below or above the average for England and Wales. Similar calculations can be done to compare disease rates, or to compare disease or death rates between years rather than between classes in any year.

If the population in 1950-1952 is taken as the standard (ie, its SMR is by definition 100), then the SMR in 1866-1870 was 349. By 1886-1890 the SMR had fallen to 300, in 1911-1915 to 205 and in 1931-1935 to 134.[6]

With advances in sanitation, environmental hygiene, occupational hygiene, nutrition and medical skills, death rates have fallen steadily to reach an SMR of 70 in 1986-1990. Yet the Registrar General's calculations have shown that from the time when the five-category classification of social class was introduced in 1921, social class inequalities in health have remained entrenched despite these advances,[7,8] as illustrated by the SMR's for men of working age in Table 1:

Table 1

Social class	1921-23	1930-32	1949-53	1959-63	1970-72	1979-80 1982-83
I	82	90	86	76	77	66
II	94	94	92	81	81	76
III	95	97	101	100	99/106	94/106
IV	101	102	104	103	114	116
V	125	111	118	143	137	165

Up to 1953, these SMR's are for men aged 20 to 64 years. After that date they are for men aged 15 to 64 years. The figures for social class III in 1970-1972 and after refer to non-manual and manual. Data for 1981 are not available. If anything, social class inequalities in health are increasing.

It is important to realise that these figures cover a period which saw the establishment of a Ministry for Health (1919), the health reforms of the 1920's and 1930's such as the Public Health (TB) Act of 1921 and the Midwives Act of 1936, a massive expansion of hospital beds in World War II and the introduction of the National Health Service in 1948. State expenditure before 1900 never exceeded £100 million. By 1979-1980 tax revenue amounted to £60.5 billion, 59% coming from income tax, 7% from taxes on company income, 2% from taxes on capital transfer (including estate duties) and 32% from taxes on commodities.[9] Total tax revenues were by this time amounting to close to 40% of the gross national product. By 1984-1985 public expenditure as a whole amounted to £126 billion, of which social security accounted for £37 billion and health and personal social services £15.4 billion. Taking per capita spending on the National Health Service in 1975 as 100, then the respective figures in 1949 and 1984 were 40 and more than 120. How can it be that increases in public expenditure on this vast scale, so much of it devoted to social security and health care, should fail completely even to begin to reduce the gap in health between the rich and poor? In approaching this question we must first ask ourselves whether the data are consistent, and whether they can be believed.

The consistency of the data

The data presented so far have referred only to total mortality in men of working age. However, social class inequalities can be shown to be present from birth through to retirement, to apply to both sexes, and to exist not only for death but also for disease and disability. Here for example is the number of deaths in the first week of life per 1000 live births according to social class in 1975 and 1990.[1] The data are from the Office of Population Censuses and Surveys:

	1975	1990
Classes I and II	15.0	6.2
Classes IV and V	22.7	9.5

Once again the results show remarkable improvement in all social classes over a 15 year period, together with an inability to reduce the social class differential. The rate for social classes IV and V was 51% higher than that for classes I and II in 1975, and 54% higher in 1990.

The baby born to a father in unskilled employment has about twice the risk of death before reaching its first birthday compared with the baby of the professional father. When births outside marriage are taken into account, the contrast is even greater. The unskilled worker and his children also run at least twice the risk of death as the professional man and his offspring. This means an average of five years less of life expectancy for the 20 year old male in social classes IV and V than for his fellow in social classes I and II.[10] These five years are retirement years for which men of all classes save in their state pension, occupational pension and national insurance schemes, but which many members of the lower classes are destined not to enjoy. If all children up to 15 years of age in England and Wales had the survival-chances of those born into social classes I and II, more than 3000 deaths might be prevented each year;[11] for the 16 to 64 year-olds, the corresponding figure is about 39,000 deaths avoided every year.[12]

The causes of death leading to the excess mortality of the lower social classes are many and varied. When Professor Peter Townsend looked at 78 categories of disease he found that the SMR's for 65 were higher in classes IV and V than in I or II during 1979-1983. Only malignant melonoma, a skin cancer linked to exposure to the sun's rays, showed the reverse trend. The same features are generally true for women.[13] Heart attacks, most cancers, strokes, accidents, mental disorders and suicides all take a greater toll among those sectors of British society who have lived in relative material deprivation. Many of these conditions are particularly common at younger ages in those belonging to the lower socio-economic groups. So when the measure of inequality employed is 'years of potential life lost' rather than the SMR, the health disadvantage of social classes IV and V becomes even more apparent.[14]

The Registrar General's data relate to deaths rather than sickness. The Health and Lifestyle Survey of the 1980's, undertaken by the Health Promotion Research Trust, was unusual because it examined the participants as well as asking them about their health, income, education, housing, and occupation.[15] A broad range of health indicators deteriorated with decreasing social class, and in some cases the gradient of decline was steep. This pattern could be demonstrated when the health measures were related to income or level of education.

Several researchers have attempted to refine the measure of material wealth by developing composite indices that include not only occupation but also car ownership, housing tenure and education. When this is done, the gradient between health and wealth is generally strengthened. When housing tenure was looked at separately, the SMR for men aged 15 to 64 years at death was 84 for owner-occupiers, as compared with 115 for those housed by their local authority (respective SMR's for women were 83 and 117). These data are for 1971-1981.[16]

Can statistics be believed?
Neither the classification of socio-economic group nor the estimate of the SMR is problem-free. As mentioned above, the re-allocation of certain occupations at each Census to alternative social classes has complicated the comparison of social classes over long periods of time. To overcome this difficulty the effect of reclassification has been repeatedly assessed by

coding individuals according to the current system and that employed at earlier Censuses. Another approach has been to confine the analysis to those occupations that have been placed consistently in the same social class for many years. When, for example, E R Pamuk used 143 such occupations to examine trends between 1921 and 1971, class inequalities were seen to be greater in 1970 than in the early years of this century. For married women there had been a similar increase in inequality between 1950 and 1970.[17]

From 1971 onwards many of the earlier problems of interpretation have been overcome by the Longitudinal Survey of the Office of Population Censuses and Surveys. The 1971 and 1981 Censuses have been used as sampling frames for this important study, which permits examination of the sequence of events occurring in a defined group of individuals over a finite period. In 1981, for the first time, information about individuals on the Census were linked to their information on previous Censuses. This allowed the circumstances of death to be related to the record of the deceased's life circumstances. In the same way, a child's birth could be related to the social and economic circumstances of the parents' earlier years. To generate a 1% sample of the population, 4 days were randomly selected in each year and the 1971 Census and National Health Service records of all individuals born on these days were 'flagged'. This 'cohort' of the population was then followed up in the 1981 Census (and the 1991 Census - results expected about 1995). The Survey has left no doubt that the contrasts in life expectancy between manual and non-manual male workers of pre-retirement age in England and Wales increased between 1976-1981 and 1981-1983. For manual occupations the SMR increased from 103 to 107 in this period, while for non-manual occupations the SMR fell from 84 to 83.[18]

The Office of Population Censuses and Surveys has since 1970 also conducted a continuous multi-purpose survey of a sample of 12,500 households who respond on a voluntary basis (response rate generally about 80%). Information is collected annually on family data, housing, employment, education and health, together with details of family income. Special topics are also selected from year to year (eg: private health insurance, source of mortgages, informal care of the sick). This survey has shown appreciably higher rates of long-term illness among manual classes than non-manual classes.[19] Furthermore, the gap between the two groups had widened between 1972 and 1978. Alongside the Health and Lifestyle Survey, which examined its participants and did not rely simply on self-report, there can be no doubt about the trends in health uncovered.

Explaining the findings

Data never lie; only their reliability and their interpretation are open to question. The implications of the findings are so far-reaching if true that they have been subject to the most severe scrutiny in recent years. Some have proposed that the inverse gradient between social class and mortality is real enough, but that it simply indicates that an individual's occupation and social class are governed by a health-selection process. In other words, those in poor health gravitate down the social scale. This suggestion harks back to 19th century concepts, as discussed later, but nevertheless must be given due consideration. Studies have shown that inter-generational social mobility is governed largely by education and family aspirations rather than health. Serious illness in childhood can have material disadvantages, but only 1% to 2% of individuals who are seriously ill in their early 20's have fallen in social class because of illness during childhood.[20] Furthermore, the illnesses that are the common causes of death today, such as coronary heart disease, cancer and stroke, rarely allow their victim time to enter employment of another kind before death. The social class gradient in death rates from lung cancer, with its short interval from diagnosis to death, is similar to that from chronic lung disease, with its many years of disability and handicap before death. If chronic lung disease commonly led to a fall in occupational standing then its associated death rate might have shown the steeper gradient with social class. Furthermore the Longitudinal Survey has found no evidence for an effect of downward mobility on the social class gradient of health in middle-age.[21] Finally, in a study of male civil servants in Whitehall, all were examined medically at recruitment and those in ill-health were excluded from follow-up. Among those clinically healthy at the start, subsequent death rates were much higher in the lower grades than in the higher grades.[22] There is therefore no evidence to believe that the relatively high mortality of social classes IV and V is explained by any tendency for the unhealthy to slide down the social scale.

Another remnant of 19th century ideas, which I discuss below, is to blame the ill-health of the lower social classes on their life-style. The implication is that these groups have choices, but that they wilfully make the wrong ones to the detriment of their own health. Certainly it is true nowadays that the lower social classes smoke more and tend to obesity more than social classes I or II, but this was not always the situation. In earlier years, the higher social classes smoked more[23] and were more corpulant than the lower classes, but the gradient between social class and mortality was in the same direction as it is today. Few dispassionate observers would be surprised if the materially disadvantaged, with their limited choices, should eat a less healthy diet and take to forms of relief ultimately more affordable for them than those selected by the upper classes. Symbols chosen by the upper social classes to signify their status often allude to possession of wealth. As such symbols are adopted by the lower social classes (perhaps because of a fall in price relative to income), the higher classes seek more expensive alternatives to take their place as fashion dictates, and with relatively little consideration for health effects (eg: a permanent sun tan).

In the study of Whitehall's civil servants, the numbers of participants were large enough to look within subgroups. Confining the analysis to non-smokers, coronary heart disease remained strongly and inversely related to grade of employment.[22] In an important study in the USA, families in Alameda County, California, have been followed since 1965. Even when the effects of smoking, drinking and race were controlled for, the poorest families still had a risk of death 50% higher than the richest families.[24]

The totality of the evidence leads to the inescapable conclusion that inequalities in health between the social classes are real and not accounted for by artefact. Ill health has its influence on occupation later on, but the effect is very small compared with the strength of the gradient between health and socio-economic status that exists in modern Britain. Nor do life-style characteristics such as smoking and diet go far enough to account for the findings. These results, coming from many and diverse studies, and the wide range of diseases and disorders that come together to increase sickness and death rates in the materially deprived, must mean that the gradient of health with social class is grounded on something as fundamental as material wealth itself. To understand the social forces that have led the country to this point, and to discover where society went wrong in its efforts to alleviate poverty and the shortfall in health that afflicts the materially deprived, we must look back over history.

2

The evolution of health care in Britain

During the 18th and 19th centuries there was continuous debate about poverty, its importance for the nation, and how the wealthy should respond to the indigent. From those times right up to the earlier years of this century, Britain has oscillated between fears of over-population and a dread that, with declining birth rates or high mortality rates, the population may be declining. Too much population growth might jeopardise the nation's self-sufficiency in food. A sick or declining population may jeopardise the nation's security by weakening its ability to defend itself. Poverty was obviously associated with disease of all kinds, and too much poverty was therefore a threat to peace and security. The poor died in large numbers whenever their malnourishment was exacerbated by poor harvests. Typhus regularly followed in the wake of bad harvests, as in 1718, 1728 and 1741.

The answer to this uncertainty seemed to be a census, as had been undertaken already by that time in Sweden and other European states, However, when Mr Thomas Potter introduced his Census Bill to parliament in 1753 it caused great consternation.[25] If the country was really weak, disclosing the numbers would encourage its enemies. Census-taking was also thought likely to incur the wrath of God, for the bible tells how King David's Census of the Hebrews was never completed because of a plague. The Rev. Richard Price's *Observations on Reversionary Accounts* set off another bout of fear when published in 1780. He claimed that through debt, disease and poverty, 'amidst all our splendours we are decreasing so fast, as to have lost, in about 70 years, near a quarter of our population'. Price saw the growing towns as the source of conditions giving rise to poverty, disease and death.[26] The comfortably situated felt a strong need to act for the security of the nation, but all of that was changed by Thomas Robert Malthus, clergyman and economist of sorts, with publication of his *Essay on the Principles of Population* in 1798.[27]

Malthus' ideas, or rather their too-ready acceptance, set back by 100 years the cause of poverty, and poverty of health. Malthus taught that populations expanded in geometric progression, doubling in size about every 25 years, whereas their subsistence could not possibly grow faster than in arithmetic progression, an increase by a constant quantity every 25 years. Since no people can exist without subsistence, nature must either cull by an increased mortality among the weak, or the people themselves must postpone reproduction. Malthus taught that famine, disease, vice and misery (the positive check) were nature's way of culling those sectors of society that bred beyond the limits of their subsistence. These ideas were fought bitterly by many, William Godwin and William Cobbett for example, but for all-too-obvious reasons the Malthusian doctrine was the preferred explanation for the existence of poverty by the affluent. It also harmonized with the theory of wages at that time, which was that they were paid from a finite amount of capital. Increasing numbers of labourers could only mean a reduction in wages. But the reasoning led to even worse conclusions. If the wealthy were to spread their wealth among the poor, nature's 'positive check' would be thwarted. The poor would reproduce even more, wages and subsistence must fall, and the outcome would be common misery and the decline of civilisation. Malthus campaigned against the Poor Law, believing that relief would encourage births among the destitute. The first edition of Malthus' book ran to 50,000 words, but so popular did it become that he was emboldened to enlarge on his doctrine. The sixth edition of 1826 ran to 225,000 words and translations appeared in several languages. Engels, describing English attitudes in the early 1840's, found the Malthusian doctrine 'the pet theory of all genuine English bourgois'.[28]

A commission appointed in 1833 to examine the administration of the Poor Law was inspired by Malthusian doctrine. Its conclusion - the system was ruining the nation. The New Poor Law, passed in 1834, was barbaric in nature. Relief in the form of money and provisions was abolished. The destitute were henceforth to be admitted to workhouses (known popularly as Poor Law Bastilles), in which conditions were made deliberately severe and repressive. Families were split up to prevent breeding. The work undertaken by the inmates was chosen so as not to compete with private enterprise; stonebreaking for men and the picking apart of old rope for oakum by the women and children.

Several philosophers and economists took up the cause of Malthus, among them Herbert Spencer (1820-1903). Spencer believed the poor to be of defective moral character. If the poor were given more than the absolute minimum, moral decline would permeate good society. Poverty was the necessary reminder to society of the consequences of laziness and lack of moral fibre.[29] When Darwin published his *Origin of Species* in 1859, his ideas about evolution in biology were immediately manipulated by Spencer to give scientific credence to his beliefs. It was Spencer who created the ideas behind 'social Darwinism'; and it was Spencer, not Darwin, who introduced the phrase 'survival of the fittest'! Victorian intelligentsia saw mankind stratified in evolutionary terms, with the aboriginal peoples at the bottom, the British upper classes at the top, and the British poor somewhere in-between. The society of William IV and Victoria promoted theories which appeared to justify the status quo with its rigid hierarchy. To show concern for the needs of the poor, even their health and high risk of premature death, was to flout the laws of God and nature, as supported by the latest of scientific ideas.

The dawn of enlightenment
There were, however, practical problems to arise from the doctrines of Malthus and Spencer. Firstly, the poor themselves and the more philanthropic among society did not see things eye-to-eye with these gentlemen. Secondly, the infectious and contagious nature of many diseases, and their links with squalor were recognised many decades before the theory of germs was promulgated. The middle and upper classes were by no means immune to the ravages of tuberculosis, typhus and smallpox. But it was the arrival of cholera in Britain that spread fear and panic across the nation. On 4 November 1831, the first case was diagnosed in Sunderland. A massive epidemic of cholera swept the country in 1832, and another in 1848-9. The population had not experienced this disease before, and its arrival brought

terror and rioting. The popular belief that it was spread by a miasma of foul air led to increasing demands for sanitary controls, water management and waste disposal. Edwin Chadwick was Secretary of the Poor Law Commission when he acted as main author of the *Report on the Sanitary Conditions of the Labouring Population of Great Britain*, published in 1842. This document, presenting the results of a study of the relations between ill-health and environmental conditions, concluded that the most important measures to be undertaken by local authorities were drainage, removal of refuse, and improvements in water supply. Parliament responded by passing the Nuisance Removal and Disease Prevention Act of 1848 to deal with the second cholera outbreak. In the same year the Public Health Act established the first General Board of Health, together with District Boards of Health wherever the Registrar General found the death rate to be above 23 per 1000.[30,31]

Pressure from public figures such as Charles Kingsley and Michael Farriday, and a better understanding of communicable diseases, led to a succession of legislative reforms concerned with slum clearance, the isolation of patients with infectious disease, and environmental sanitation. The Public Health Acts of 1872 and 1875 defined local authority responsibility for sanitary measures and established effective measures which saw mortality rates fall from 22 per 1000 in 1871-1875 to 17.7 per 1000 in 1896-1900.[6]

These actions were all put on a more scientific footing with the growth of the science of bacteriology following the identification of the organism responsible for anthrax by Koch in 1876. Of every 1000 deaths in males between 1848 and 1872, 146 had been caused by tuberculosis and 13 were from smallpox. By 1900, the respective numbers were 84 for tuberculosis and 1 for smallpox.[32] Around 1870, children aged 5 to 9 years were dying annually at a rate of 7/1000, but by 1900 this had fallen to 4/1000.[6] In 1880, however, the Malthusian doctrine was still so strongly held by many of the intelligentsia that Henry George felt compelled to devote no fewer than 4 chapters of his best seller, *Progress and Poverty* (1879), in refutation.[33]

The health of the poor
The poor had traditionally sought care for sickness in the voluntary hospitals maintained by the monastic institutions and other charities. By the

middle 1800's they could handle only a minority of cases. For example in 1861, there were 50,000 sick paupers in the wards of the workhouses, and 11,000 patients in the voluntary hospitals. It was partly to deal with the sheer numbers of the sick that two Acts of the 1860's required local authorities to establish isolation hospitals, fever hospitals and mental asylums. But the New Poor Law held its grip, and there was to be no relief for the underlying poverty. Even in 1900 the elderly poor were still carried to the workhouse by their sons and daughters.

In the 1870's the data in the General Register Office were first put to an examination of death rates within the strata of British Society. In 1874, Charles Ansell tabulated the mortality experience of the upper and professional classes. Of every 100 children born to peerage families, about 12 would not survive to 10 years of age. For the upper classes the respective number was 15, and for the general population, about 30. In 1887, Noel Humphrey, Assistant Registrar General, stated that it was 'urgently desirable that we should know more about the rates of mortality prevailing in the different strata of society'. Essentially nothing more was done in this regard, however, until Dr Stevenson's tabulations of 1911, as noted earlier.[4]

British Society at the turn of the century
The industrial revolution and the Victorian expansion of Empire made London the financial centre of world trade. The huge increase in wealth and opportunity were most unequally shared between the classes, the regions and the sexes. The newly rich through trade and industry aspired to and were drawn into the ranks of the older landed aristocracy, acquiring land themselves. By 1900 the new upper class was an amalgam served in the House of Commons by 250 bankers, merchants, company directors and other leaders of trade, together with 70 Lords, Baronets and other titled personages. The limitation of franchise meant that political divides were more on religious lines than class lines at this time, in the shape of the Conservative and Liberal wings of the middle and upper classes. The Independent Labour Party did not exist until 1893. Full manhood suffrage had to wait until 1918; at the turn of the century only about 60% of British men had the vote, and the 40% without were mostly working class. Enfranchisement for women was not completed until 1928, and even up to

the launching of the National Health Service in 1948, businessmen and university graduates had two votes to everyone-else's one. The lower socio-economic classes had little or no political influence over their own status or health until after 1918; they took what they were given. England was in those days a very good place for gentlemen, whose comfort rested on an unlimited and cheap supply of labour, especially in domestic service, and an income tax so moderate as to be almost negligible.

Two themes came to dominate politics in Britain over the period 1890-1910 (along with other issues such as Free Trade), both of fundamental importance for this analysis. One was a developing programme of personal social services for the alleviation of the worst effects of poverty and the control of disease; the other was the means for financing this programme.

Development of Personal Social Services
Public opinion came more and more to believe that high death rates in infancy and childhood were not inevitable dictates of nature, and that poverty and squalor were at the root of much of it. By the end of the nineteenth century, Sir John Simon, Medical Officer to the Privy Council, was able to refer to poverty as 'among the worst of sanitary evils.'[34] From 1890 onwards pressure began to grow for measures to intervene against poverty and ill-health at a personal level as well as at the level of public health. The first sign of movement in this direction came with the Workmen's Compensation Act of 1897, under which the employer was considered to be liable for the results of industrial injury.

The South African war of 1899-1902 provided a further jolt to the public consciousness when about half the working men who volunteered for active service had to be rejected because of ill health, mainly poor physical development, heart disease and poor eyesight. There were also reports detailing the poor physical health of adolescents seeking work in factories. A subsequent Inter-Departmental Committee on Physical Deterioration recommended that schoolchildren should be inspected medically at frequent intervals; and that school meals should be organised by local authorities. Here then was the cradle of the 'reactive' approach to the ill-health among the materially deprived, legislation directing local authority services to alleviate suffering from which the poor were unable to relieve themselves.

At this time the only public medical service outside the voluntary hospitals was that under the Poor Law. The working population was slowly increasing and life expectancy was growing, and the infirmary wings of the workhouses could not cope with demand. Two thirds of the sick were in these institutions; understaffed, unspecialised, and with no visiting physicians or surgeons. Poor Law district medical officers offered a rudimentary domiciliary service, but they were underpaid, disliked by private physicians, and were not expected to advise on disease prevention. The Poor Law system came to be regarded as quite inadequate, and so a Royal Commission was set up between 1905 and 1909 to examine its operation. The majority of the Commissioners were concerned to find ways to improve its operation. Among measures proposed were the transfer of responsibility from the Poor Law Guardians to county and county borough councils, the replacement of the workhouse infirmary by specialised institutions, and the creation of dispensaries with attendant doctors for the low-paid, on payment of a subscription.[35] A minority report, whose best known authors were Beatrice Webb and George Lansbury, wanted abolition of the Poor Law and attention to the causes of poverty.[36]

The Liberals were swept to power in a landslide victory of 1906, with Campbell-Bannerman as Prime Minister. He made clear the Party's intentions for social and financial reforms. The social programme was to be funded in large measure from site-value taxation, or as he put it, by making the land 'more of a treasure house for the nation'.[37] Asquith replaced the ailing Prime Minister in 1908, and chose Lloyd-George for his Chancellor of the Exchequer. Lloyd-George was an ardent land reformer, and a man who believed that poverty was caused by a lack of opportunity for work, sickness and old age. In 1908 the Government introduced the Old Age Pensions Act which provided for a fixed weekly sum out of central taxation for all persons aged 70 years or more who satisfied certain requirements (7s 6d for a married couple). Then in 1911 came the National Health Insurance Bill, introducing a public scheme paid for in part by insurance contributions. The aim was to relieve poverty among workers with incomes of less than £160/year (gradually raised to £420/year by 1942) by providing a sickness allowance and a minimum medical care service (not covering dependents).

This approach to poverty through relief had a long and very understandable precedent. During the 17th century, at a time when people were rendered destitute mostly by natural disaster or personal misfortune (famine, flood, disease, accident), the reactive response was logical even if very inadequate. The voluntary hospitals and the charitable actions of medical men likewise were humane and indispensable responses to the suffering of the poor. There were those in the late nineteenth century, however, who had come to recognise that by that time by no means all poverty and disease was the result of natural disaster or personal misfortune. They saw that much of the social ills around them were now man-made, a consequence of the political economy, and they doubted whether in these circumstances the "reactive" approach to poverty and its consequences amounted to an effective response.

These reactive responses to society's ills needed finance, and here also the precedents had been set long previously. The Poor Law was financed through parish relief, and then eventually through larger local authorities. Income tax was introduced as a temporary measure during the Napoleonic Wars at the beginning of the nineteenth century, and became a permanent and growing feature of the tax system in 1842.[38] The initial imposition of 7d in the pound (3%) was varied subsequently to reach a peak of 7% on annual incomes of £100 or more during the Crimean War of 1854-1856. At this time, however, there were less than 500,000 taxpayers in a population of 12 million persons aged over 15 years. In his budget of 1909, Lloyd-George relied mainly on the standard forms of taxation to finance his social programme (though he would have preferred otherwise). He introduced 'progressivity' into income taxation, with a 'supertax' of 1s 8d (8%) in the pound on incomes of over £5000 per year (more than £100,000/year at current values). The increases in income tax were expected to raise an extra £3.5 million, those on estate duties a further £2.85 million, and licences and taxes on tobacco and liquor an additional £6 million. At this time there were fewer than 1.5 million taxpayers in a total population of just over 40 million, and since the large majority of the working population was not contributing, income tax could be regarded as genuinely redistributive.

The Alternative Solution
Not everybody, even in the late 19th century, accepted the principles that had led to relief of poverty in the ways employed at that time. An emerging body of opinion, largely in and around the Liberal Party, was promoting the

idea of some form of land tax for central revenue after 1880. State expenditure was less than £100 millions at that time, and some, particularly the advocates of the philosophy of Henry George, realised that a 100% 'tax' on the annual site value of land would cover this amount and leave a respectable surplus as a fund for social improvements. All taxes could therefore be replaced by a 'single tax', a phrase that gained rapidly in popularity not only among the Liberals after 1888, but also among the labouring classes and their organisations. Sidney and Beatrice Webb recorded how the philosophy of Henry George had completely changed the attitudes of urban workers by the 1890's. The old Chartist cry of 'Back to the Land' was replaced by a call for 'the unearned income of land - site value rating'.[39] Gladstone's Liberal government of 1892 championed land reform, but lacking an overall majority and faced with enormous opposition from the Conservatives in the Commons and the Lords, could achieve very little. Sir William Harcourt was, however, able to introduce a death duty on landed property at a rate of 8% in 1894.

The liberals wanted to shift the tax-base onto rent, but this required a preliminary valuation of the nation's land, and here was the stumbling block. Two Bills introduced for this purpose in 1907 and 1908 were wrecked by the Lords. To circumvent this difficulty, Lloyd-George determined to incorporate proposals for land valuation in his budget of 1909. He proposed 1d in the pound (later dropped to °d or 0.2%) on the capital value of undeveloped land and a 20% duty on the incremental value of land when sold or inherited. These new land measures, though sufficient only to raise £500,000 and hardly amounting to any meaningful tax on land values, were nevertheless the thin end of the wedge for the Conservative opposition and provoked a famous constitutional crisis. The Finance Bill did not reach its third reading until November of 1909, only to be wrecked by the Lords, so precipitating the general election of January 1910. This time the budget, with its land-valuation provisions, passed the Lords, after which the Government introduced its Parliament Bill to curb the powers of the Upper House, especially those over Finance Bills. Another rejection by the Lords led to another election at the end of 1910. Finally the Conservative's majority in the Lords decided upon abstention, and the Parliament Bill was passed.

Nearly 5000 land valuers were set to work, but Lloyd-George did not see completion of their task before 1915. His 1914 Budget statement prepared the way for a Bill to value land and improvements separately for local (but not national) purposes. A Ministry of Lands was under consideration when all was disrupted by the outbreak of war. During 1914-1918 the Government was forced once again to rely on enormous increases in income tax, with top rates in excess of 50%. After the war these rates fell back, but never again to pre-war levels. By the Finance Act of 1920 the obligation to complete the valuation of all land in the United Kingdom ceased.[40] Thus a concerted attempt to remove poverty by collecting revenue for central purposes from site-values failed. Instead, the events of 1909 to 1911 set the stage for the evolution of welfare capitalism as we know it today.

The National Health Service
In many ways, the outline of the National Health Service of 1948 onwards was laid down by the Consultative Council on Medical and Allied Services appointed by the first Minister of Health, then Dr Christopher Addison, under the chairmanship of the future Lord Dawson, as part of national reconstruction after 1918.[41] Medical knowledge was expanding and treatment becoming more specialised, making extended organisation essential. The system proposed had five forms of service, namely domiciliary, primary health centres (the forerunner of the group general practice plus cottage hospital), secondary health centres (district general hospitals), supplementary services (special institutions for fevers etc), and teaching hospitals. The service would be administered at local authority level, co-ordinated by the Ministry of Health. Owing to the state of the economy in the early 1920's, however, nothing was done to implement these suggestions. Voluntary hospitals were to continue, with central grants at times of financial crisis.

Over the following 20 years there was some growth and development, but the pattern of services changed little and co-ordination and co-operation was patchy. A report from the Hospital Almoners Association disclosed that in 1939 conditions were almost everywhere poor, but more so in the North than in the South. Shortages of specialist services were very evident, and costs for the non-insured delayed diagnosis and treatment.[42] An editorial in *The Lancet* summarised the position in the following way:

> Even before the war, there were voices crying in the wilderness that all was not well with the medical services. The burden of their cries was that

preventable diseases are not being prevented; that the chances of avoiding
death in infancy, in childbirth, from tuberculosis, and from rheumatic
carditis were much greater among the rich than the poor; that for most of
the population such financial burdens were added to the burdens of ill
health as to discourage early treatment; that the standards of treatment
available in different places and institutions, and among different social
classes, varied enormously; and that the annual income of those who cared
for the sick ranged from £40 plus keep and laundry paid to the probationer
nurse to the £40,000 earned by the successful surgeon.[43]

In 1939, a married woman had no access to free medical attention unless
she was pregnant or had recently given birth. Her children of school age
came under the care of the school medical inspector. Many women would
not 'start a doctor's bill' if they could possibly remain on their feet. Health
standards in many families were very low, and the plight of the elderly
infirm was pitiable. The intention was for the National Health System to
correct this situation.

Plans for a comprehensive health service evolved over the years 1939 to
1948. Discussions involved the Ministry of Health (which was hoping to
move towards a comprehensive medical service), the general practitioners
through the British Medical Association (which was concerned to retain
payment of doctors by a capitation fee through the National Insurance
System rather than by a salaried service), representatives of the Local
Authorities, and the voluntary hospitals. Much time was spent by the
Minister of Health trying to reconcile the differences between the various
parties. In December 1942, however, the Beveridge report was published.[44]
The Beveridge committee, with Beveridge as chairman and senior civil
servants from government departments that administered the various forms
of social security at that time, had been asked for recommendations on their
integration and possible extension. They proposed a single universal social
security scheme covering loss of earnings through sickness and disability,
unemployment or old age, with flat rate contributions and benefits and
additional assistance based on a means test, all administered by a Ministry
of Social Security. The report also included the famous 'Assumption B',
that there would be a comprehensive health service available to all and
divorced of any conditions of insurance contributions. Without such a
service, the social security system would flounder. Doctors, however,

wanted an income limit for eligibility to protect private practice, voluntary hospitals were concerned to maintain their status, and the medical profession in general did not want local authority control. The matter eventually reached Cabinet and a White Paper on a National Health Service appeared in 1944, as a consultative document. The objective was stated quite clearly. 'The Government want to ensure that in future every man and woman and child can rely on getting all the advice and treatment and care which they may need in matters of health; that what they get shall be the best medical and other facilities available; that their getting them shall not depend on whether they can pay for them, or any other factor irrelevant to the real need - the real need being to bring the country's full resources to bear upon reducing ill-health and promoting good health in all its citizens.'[45]

The costs of this service were to be borne very largely through central and local taxation. These were estimated at £132 millions compared with £54.5 millions in 1938-1939 for an incomplete service. Average wages in 1939 were £180 per year, and there were fewer than four million taxpayers at that time in a working population of more than 20 million. Clearly therefore, the Government saw the health service as a means of redistribution of wealth in kind to benefit the health of the lower social classes. The service was envisaged to pay for itself by reducing sickness rates and thereby the need for social security, and by lowering the economic waste of premature disability and death.

The Labour government was swept to power in July 1945, with Aneurin Bevan as Minister of Health. The first task was to decide on the organisation and administration of hospitals, which the wartime caretaker government had struggled with for some time. Bevan's answer was straightforward; all hospitals should be taken into national ownership and administered by local bodies with delegated powers. Financing of the scheme was planned only partly through National Health Insurance (to become simply National Insurance), amounting to £35.7 millions, the Exchequer contributing £103.3 millions and the local rates £6.0 millions.[46] Bevan's National Health Service Bill of March 1946 revealed a tripartite structure. The Minister would be directly responsible for hospitals and specialist services, but would act through new regional and local bodies. County and County Borough authorities would be responsible for health centres, clinics and domiciliary services. Executive Councils, half professional and half lay, would administer general practitioner services of doctor, dentist and pharmacist.

Between 1946 and 5 July 1948 when, with the National Insurance Scheme, the National Health Service became a reality, an immense amount of administrative re-organisation was undertaken against bitter opposition from the British Medical Association. Bevan steered a course through this resistance and doubts among the Cabinet, with the support of the Royal College of Physicians.

The National Health Service has been in many ways an undoubted success compared with the pre-war situation. It took the commercial element out of medicine. Doctors could practice without considerations of profit or the patient's financial losses. The hospital system was improved immensely. It operated in tandem with national insurance to offer security against the immediate distress of unemployment and illness. However, the principle that the health service should be provided free at the time of need was soon breached in minor ways and has repeatedly been under threat over the past 35 years. Prescription charges, dental charges and opticians' charges have all come about partly to raise revenue and partly to deter abuse. In reality of course, the service was never 'free' but paid for by taxation of wages and interest. Since 1960, essentially the whole working population of Britain has been eligible for taxation and, through various adjustments to income tax rates, progressivity has been diminished. Furthermore, the introduction of value-added tax firstly at rates of 8% and 12.5%, later at a single higher rate of 15%, has made the tax system even less progressive. The 1979 Report of the Royal Commission on Income and Wealth disclosed that between 1949 and 1979, the share of total 'after tax' income taken by the top 10% of income earners fell only from 27.1% to 23.4%, and over the same period the share taken by the bottom 30% also fell from 14.6% to 12.1%.[47]

The Family Expenditure Survey has shown that in 1986, income-in-kind from use of the National Health Service amounted on average to £910 for families in the bottom 20% in terms of original income (ie, income from employment, occupational pensions, gifts and investments). For the top 20%, the average was £710. For housing subsidies, the respective incomes-in-kind averaged £130 and £20. For educational services the gradient was reversed; £270 for the bottom fifth and £850 for the top fifth.[48]

The Black Report
In March 1977, David Ennals, Secretary of State for Social Services, drew attention to what he called the 'worrying' differences in mortality rates between the social classes. He considered attempts to narrow this gap in health standards a major challenge for the next decade. Accordingly, he appointed a Research Working Group, chaired by the President of the Royal College of Physicians (Sir Douglas Black), to examine the evidence and draw implications for policy. Its work was completed in 1980, by which time there had been a change of Government. It concluded that the social class differences were not only real but sharpening, that they accounted for the loss of tens of thousands of lives each year, and that something had gone wrong with the system of social welfare.[7]

The report argued that the National Health Service was not to blame, for much of the problem lay with social and economic factors beyond its influence. A call was made for more research and information on the problem, together with radical improvement of the material conditions of society's poorer groups. Here, however, it could only suggest more of the same. About half of its recommendation related to the delivery of care, while the rest sought improvements in living standards through increases in child benefit, maternity grants, disability allowances, provision for infant care, free school meals, housing grants and so on.

The report did not find favour with the Conservative Government, which declined to grant it even the usual publication through Her Majesty's Stationery Office. The Secretary of State calculated that the extra tax burden imposed by the recommendations would amount to more than £2 billion per year, more than the country could afford in the economic climate at that time. He was also wholly unconvinced that the effectiveness of what was being proposed was established. Thus the review and its recommendations were dismissed and the matter was left unattended. Sir George Young, the then Under-Secretary of State for Health and Security, saw progress being made by encouraging health education (first stressed in the Dawson report of 1920), personal responsibility for health (going back even further to 19th century notions), and encouraging voluntary organisations (an approach known to lead to disorganisation and inefficiency, as during the inter-war years).[49] Yet in a way the Government was right to be suspicious of the report's recommendations. Where was the evidence from past experience that they would work?

Conclusions

Eighty years is more than long enough to conclude from Britain's vital statistics that the nation's system of personal social security and health care has failed to achieve its primary objectives. Social class differences in death rates, as measured by their SMR's, are much the same today as they were in the 1920's. This is because relative shortfalls in health are fundamentally inseparable from shortfalls in material wealth. Britain's ever increasingly complex system of taxation of wages and interest (here used in the classical sense of the returns to capital) has largely failed to redistribute wealth from the richer to the poorer sectors of society, and its national health service has been unable to protect the materially deprived from the consequent adverse effects on their health. Looking back to the origins of the welfare system, we can see how between 1890-1910 there was a great debate about the proper source of public revenue to pay for the programme of personal social services that was in its embryonic stages at that time. One school promoted the taxation of wages and interest; the other wished to collect the economic rent of land for this purpose. The former emerged victorious but, as we now see, to the detriment of the health of the nation. The vast accumulation of wealth and general improvement in the standard of living during the 20th century has not been accompanied by any improvement in the shortfall of health among the lower social classes. We must therefore look again at the proposals of those who sought to reap the site value of the land to ensure a greater equity in the distribution of the nation's wealth for the public good.

3

Back to Basics

The relative wealth held by the rich and the poor is difficult to quantify unlike their life expectancy. For our purposes, however, this is not required, but for the discussion of the creation and distribution of wealth that follows it is necessary to define our terms - the need for which is explained in *The Corruption of Economics* in this series. Wealth comprises all natural resources secured and modified by productive labour for the gratification of human desires. As such, it does not include mediums to facilitate its exchange, such as money. The three elements in the production of wealth always have been and always will be land, labour and capital. Land encompasses all opportunities for wealth-creation provided by nature, and excludes any improvements to land through the application of labour and capital. Such improvements are themselves capital when applied to the production in wealth. Labour is the application of human exertion, mental and physical, to land for the creation of wealth. Capital is wealth set aside to assist labour in the creation of further wealth.

The exchange of capital for real property causes an elementary failure in the minds of many to distinguish clearly between land and capital. In this exchange, part of the capital is exchanged for buildings, services and other improvements, the value of which depreciates over time without further investment. The remainder of the capital exchanged is for the site value of the land, which is independent of the improvements. It is the site value, and not the improvements, which increases during a 'house'-price 'boom' for example. Use of the term 'real property', without recognising its two mutually exclusive elements, land and capital, impedes progress in economic thought in a way as fundamental as would speaking of 'water', if its elemental constituents, hydrogen and oxygen, were ignored in chemistry.

The forces governing site values are fundamental to any discussion of inequality in wealth, and are considered below.

No matter how complicated the economy becomes, no matter how fine the division of labour, how numerous the exchanges in the conversion of raw material to the finished product, how many the inventions, or how great the variety of finished products that constitute wealth, the elements upon which the economy is built remain land, labour and capital. Material advancement, both per capita and in aggregate, depends upon growth of the working population, improvements in the means of production and exchange, and certain features of social organisation that are conducive to wealth creation (eg, good government). In a free economy where laws and regulations do not create biases such as restrictions, privilege or monopoly, there will be no hindrance to gainful employment, a gradual increase in per capita wealth and with it general improvements in health. The question arises as to what happens to the distribution of this wealth with material progress, for it is the distribution of wealth that is of concern here.

The distribution of wealth
Land, labour and capital share in the wealth that they combine to produce. That proportion going to land is (economic) rent, that to labour is wages and that to capital is interest. The meaning of these terms differ somewhat from common usage. Rent is that part of wealth going to land in return for the use of natural opportunities, wages that part going to labour as the reward for human exertion, and interest that part returned to capital for its use. Rent as defined is not to be confused with commercial rent, which like other forms of 'profit', is a mixture of economic rent, interest and wages. Of course, an individual can receive income from any combination of these sources, but when thinking of economy in society we must collect all rent, all wages and all interest into three separate aggregates in order to understand what is happening.

Land, labour and capital each seek to maximise their proportion of total wealth. Production requires the exertion of labour on land, but there is a minimum return for exertion on marginal land of low productivity below which labour will find itself losing rather than benefiting. What this minimum wage is we do not need to consider here, but it is evidently a function of the general level of prosperity and is much higher now than in the 19th century. This basic wage constitutes the margin of productivity. Labour on marginal land receives only a minimum wage, but what it creates it keeps as there is no excess that can be taken in rent. Since marginal land produces no rent, it has no site value (for site value is only rent capitalised), but more productive land will generate more wealth for the same application, and this excess can be taken in rent. Thus as the productivity of labour and capital increases, whether the result of increasing population, invention or improved organisation, an increasing proportion of the wealth created goes to rent, and though wages and interest may increase absolutely, they decline as a proportion of total wealth. This is a fundamental economic principle called Ricardo's law of rent, which states:

> The rent of land is determined by the excess of its produce over that which the same application of labour and capital can secure from the least productive land in use.

One illustration of this phenonomenon is supplied by a comparison of average wages and average house prices. With increasing national wealth over the long-term, the ratio of house prices to wages gradually increases.

The inequitable treatment of rent
So far, this account of economic phenomena seems natural enough and no problem has been identified. In the case of Britain and similar economies, however, we now begin to perceive the fundamental flaw in the existing system which acts as a sink, extracting wealth from labour and capital as material prosperity rises, thereby distorting its equitable distribution. This sink is created by legal and fiscal institutions which permit the appropriation of rent by landowning interests rather than its return to society as a whole. The fundamental principles that no return is due without exertion, and that living on the labour of others is immoral, evidently do not apply to those who hold title to land. The more effective labour and capital become, the greater the proportion of the income that is taken by the landholder in rent. Part of this maldistribution has become obscured by the ensuing redistribution policies that were ostensibly designed to compensate for the socio-economic friction to which it has given rise. Nevertheless, those classes of citizen having nothing but their labour, by and large the lower socio-economic groups (the bottom 50% in Britain's table of wealth own less than 1% of

all land),[50] remain seriously handicapped; for the more productive is their exertion the less is the proportionate return to them owing to increases both in rent and tax. The fact that wages may have risen absolutely can soothe, even beguile, for while labour may be aware of increases in taxation which reduce the purchasing power of wages, it fails to notice the increasing inequalities in the distribution of wealth.

Equitable forms of wealth distribution
There is a justifiable distribution of wages about the average. Individuals who are particularly productive because of innate ability, special skills or knowledge, a creative application to work, or successful risk-taking earn a commensurate increase in their return for exertion which is generally acknowledged as fair. On the other hand, there are individuals who through misfortune such as illness, accident, or natural disaster are ineffective creators of wealth (at worst, totally dependent). Here is the rightful place for health and social care services, insurance, and charitable works, the marks of civilised society. This differential in productivity between individuals explains the distribution of wages within occupations and across society (for it partly explains social mobility). However, when labour is generally successful and the average level of wealth creation increases, then the proportion of wealth going to rent rises. Thus whereas the distributive effects of individual effort are equitable, this is not the case once the existing tax and tenure arrangements affect the distribution of income that flows from a general increase in productivity. The private appropriation of the additional rent that has been generated is a basic injustice. It is a remedy for this inequitable component that is needed if significant inroads are to be made in redressing socio-economic differences that give rise to inequalities in health.

Charity and welfare services applied to alleviate deprivation arising from the inequitable component of wealth distribution are currently necessary, but while relieving acute distress they also serve to deflect attention from root causes. These reactive approaches also assume, probably simplistically, that the problem is entirely one of material poverty. There may well be additional psycho-social dimensions to subhealth, morbidity and mortality having origins in the same system responsible for the inequitable distribution of wealth, dimensions which the 'welfare' approach may unwittingly entrench.

A remedy
Corrective action must start with the acknowledgement that, under the present tax-and-tenure arrangements, labour and capital are vulnerable to the systemic increase in rent. For those with little or no entitlement to rent (a characteristic of the lower socio-economic classes) this distortion matters a great deal. Of the many political economists to consider this problem, perhaps the most incisive was Henry George.[33] He proposed that rent be collected for central government revenue, to ease the burden of taxation on wages and interest and return to the community what the community has created.

To say as some opponents of this fiscal policy argue, that the separation of the site value from the value of the improvements (a necessary step before collecting rent for the community) is too difficult is an affront to intelligence. Every day, derelict land is valued in the urban sprawl, the values of sites are assessed after destructive fires and so on.

What is proposed calls not for any massive and 'reactive' increase in expenditure. Neither does it seek to bolster the income of the materially deprived by taxing the wages of the more successful among labour (to the possible detriment to the health of the latter it has even been claimed). Rather, the remedy is to remove taxes from all labour and capital by shifting the tax base onto the rent of land. Income gained inequitably, even if good for your health, cannot morally be held at the expense of the health of others!

Some mechanisms that link land policy and health
a) Housing
On his installation to Glasgow University in 1883, John Bright referred to the 1881 census, noting with dismay that about 30% of families in Scotland lived in one room, and 40% in two rooms. With the generation of wealth since that time, the Victorian slums are no more, and by 1981 only 1% of Scotland's households were overcrowded according to the legal definition of the term.[51] Nevertheless, serious deficiencies in housing have endured, a sizeable proportion of the housing stock remaining below a tolerable standard.[52] In Scotland for example, 21% of houses are affected by damp, condensation or mould (many will be cold and draughty).[53] In selected areas

of our major cities almost half of all families live in rooms affected by mould.[54]

Adults unable to escape poor housing suffer excessively from nausea, vomiting, nasal obstruction, dyspnoea, backache, fainting and 'bad nerves'; their children from wheezing, sore throat, headache, fever, cough and nasal discharge, even after allowance for income, cigarette smoking, unemployment and overcrowding.[54] Effects of such conditions on mental health are difficult to disentangle from those of other factors commonly endured by those in bad housing, such as low status, feelings of alienation and neglect, and financial anxieties, but few would seriously doubt that poor housing can contribute to anxiety - depression. So what prevents the nation, and in particular its building industry, from responding effectively to the need for better housing? The fundamental reason is the treatment of land.

Housebuilding is the most immediately vulnerable of all industries to land speculation; investment in this sector is more unstable than in the manufacturing sector,[55] as illustrated by events in the 1970's and 1980's.[56] Between 1956 and 1974, the average price of a new building on mortgage increased by more than 400%, while basic weekly wages in manufacturing rose by only 215% and gross company trading profits by 236%. Since home price increases outstripped building costs, building site values increased by much more than 400%. Betwen 1970 and 1973, the average price of a plot soared from £907 to £2676, and the ratio of house prices to earnings increased from 3.3 to 4.8. The effect was to reduce the spending power of wages after mortgages were financed. The resultant decline in demand for articles from the manufacturing sector forced reductions in stock and the workforce.

In a free market economy, the high cost of building land in 1973 could be put down simply to supply and demand; no more than the difference between building costs and what buyers were freely willing to pay for title. But there is not a free market in land. The rapid acceleration in house prices represented no more than a spate of speculation, throwing the economy out of tune. Those monopolising the land were effectively forcing prices up by restraining the supply to the market. Predictably, prices collapsed in 1974, and by 1976 the ratio of house prices to earnings was back to 3.51. In 1977, building was still depressed but land prices started to escalate once more.

Builders could not obtain land and make a realistic return, given the disposable income of households at that time. Responding to complaints, the Housing Minister declared, 'The message for the building industry .... is that competition is both the key to success and the only guarantee of survival.'[57] Forced to compete for land at speculative prices, builders were the major casualties in the 20% increase in bankruptcies heard in the London High Court during 1981. The state of the industry since that time is common knowledge.

At the extreme, high rents and lack of affordable housing culminate in homelessness (2 million in Britain today) with its own deleterious effects on health.[58] Yet the building industry is more than up to the task of revitalising the housing stock, and there is no shortage of land. Indeed, the Civic Trust found in 1977 that 137,000 acres of England and Wales were officially derelict. An additional 250,000 acres stood 'dormant' (undamaged but idle) - an area larger than Birmingham, Glasgow, Liverpool and Manchester combined.[59] What happened in the 1970's and the 1980's, as on many earlier occasions, was a forcing of rent by the creation of an artificial scarcity. Sir Peter Trench, a leading expert in UK housing, concluded that, 'By the end of the 1980's, the need for new housing would continue well in advance of supply. Supply, because of land, will be in a thorough mess!'[60]

b) Employment
An inability to find gainful employment has many adverse consequences for both worker and dependents, and employment is affected by the land policy in several ways. In Britain in the late 1970's, construction directly employed 1.25 million and represented 11% of the gross national product. In addition, hundreds of thousands were employed in dependent industries. Thus, the consequences of land speculation for employment in the building and related industries are readily appreciated. In 1981, over 300,000 of the unemployed were construction workers. Speculation in land reduces capital available for productive purposes, and the lack of such funds forces businesses to reduce stock and cut back on the workforce. Many small businesses rent their premises, and when new leases are negotiated, the increases can be seriously disruptive.

The exclusion of rent from taxation has its own detrimental effects on employment. The displacement of tax onto labour and capital for central government revenue combines to create high labour costs with reduced purchasing power of wages. The worker is unemployable if deemed incapable of producing goods and services to the costs of the labour plus taxes (income tax, value-added tax, national insurance). This is the 'tax wedge' between labour and employment. Attempts to encourage employment by lowering taxes on capital fail in large measure because of the land policy, as illustrated by the history of 'enterprise' zones. The 'tax breaks' offered to entrepreneurs willing to move to such zones were immediately swallowed in increased rent. Thus when government created such zones in 1981, rents rose by up to 50% as compared with those for sites just beyond their boundaries. What was meant for capital and labour was largely seized by land.[61] The investment attracted was not capital or labour intensive - warehousing was the favoured means of extracting the increased land-rent.

Speaking of Britain during the 1970's, Margaret Thatcher said, 'We got an artificial boom, and do you know where the money went? It did not go into investment or expansion; it went into the biggest property boom we've ever seen and I don't wish to see the like of it ever again. It did the Conservative Party immense harm, it not only went into these enormous increases in property, the boom eventually collapsed, and in the meantime inflation rose and rose and eventually unemployment rose again ......'.[62] The consequences of unemployment for health are well recognised. Children of the unemployed show deficits in growth and development compared with those of the employed within each social class.[63,64] Men who were seeking work in the week preceding the 1981 Census were found to have a significantly excessive mortality in 1983 due predominantly to lung cancer, coronary heart disease, accidents and violence. Their excess death rate was not explained by their pre-existing health or their socio-economic status before unemployment.[65] Others have reported an association between unemployment and an increased mortality from coronary heart disease.[66]

The anxiety and depression going with the threat of unemployment, or its realisation, are only too readily understood.[67] One of the tools of research into psychological health is known as the general health questionnaire, which contains questions on loss of sleep, lack of concentration, feelings of depression, sense of self-worth, and worry. With this measure the unemployed score far worse than the employed.[68] Follow-up studies have shown that unemployment leads to a deterioration in mental health and re-employment to improvement, regardless of sex, ethnic group or educational qualifications.[69]

In another approach, the American sociologist Harvey Brenner sought correlations between economic activity and admission rates to mental hospitals in New York State between 1841 and 1971.[70] Brenner found that instabilities in the national economy were the single most important source of fluctuation in admission rates to these hospitals. Brenner is at pains to stress that this pattern may not be confined to the unemployed - recessions may take their toll even among those who are not made redundant. His methods have been disputed, but the overall evidence leads to the not so surprising conclusion that loss of earnings and insecurity through unemployment is bad for mental health. Arguments about how the association with poor health arises, whether through loss of work per se, or loss of income, are of interest but of no relevance for our present purposes.

Time for Action
Speaking in Burlington, Iowa in 1885, Henry George stated that, 'The peculiar characteristic of this modern poverty of ours is that it is deepest where wealth is most abundant'; and elsewhere in the same speech, 'Poverty is worse than cholera; poverty kills more people than pestilence, even in the best of times. Look at the death statistics of our cities: see where the deaths come quickest.......'.[71] Compare these remarks with those of Lord Kilmarnock to the House of Lords in 1987; 'Just as the gap between the richest and poorest has increased with an overall increased national income and the plight of the homeless has become worse within an overall pattern of increased home-ownership, so health inequalities have increased .... It is all part of the same pattern'.[72] Such similar sentiments expressed by informed men one century apart, albeit in different style, are eloquent testimony to the failure of society to come to grips with the inequitable element in the distribution of its wealth and its consequences for health. The 'reactive' policies have evidently failed to achieve anything like the improvements in the health of the nation that are needed. The problem facing the pre-emptive approach proposed, however, is not one of lack of intellectual support,[73-80] but rather the lack of a 'critical mass' of political will.

The 'Black' Report has called among other measures for a fairer distribution of resources to raise the living standards of the disadvantaged and thereby improve their standard of health.[7] There will always be an unequal but nevertheless equitable distribution of wages according to an individual's productive capacity. Far more important, however, is the persistent inequitable component to the distribution of wealth that has its roots in the institutionalised appropriation of rent. Site values and rent originate not from the exertion of the landowner, but from the productivity of labour and capital when applied to land. The ever increasing share of wealth going in rent to the landowner as labour and capital increase productivity deprives the latter of an equitable access to the products of their exertion. This arrangement is obsolescent.

Britain's political economy is based upon a pre-industrial system of land tenure onto which has been grafted an industrial application of labour and capital. The failure of this hybrid to sustain full vigour arises primarily not so much from any serious deficiencies in the graft, but from the inadequacy of its rootstock. It is the latter which is mainly responsible for the recurrent depressions, protracted bouts of high unemployment and the inequalities in the distribution of wealth that in diverse ways undermine the health and wealth of the nation. The remedy is to restructure fiscal policy on the basis that people should pay for the benefits they receive. The occupation of land provides access to services provided by the community; these services are, in fact, what gives land its value. Therefore, occupiers should pay rent to defray the cost of those services. This revenue would then permit a reduction in the general level of taxation.

Apart from the equity and efficiency benefits of this approach to public finance, other benefits would follow. These would be discouragement of speculation in land, improvement in prospects of employment, and increases in net wages and personal status. On the evidence to persist with the present system of capitalist welfare offers little real prospect of a remedy. The fear is that, with increasing disillusionment, society may slip back into its old ways reminiscent of 50 years ago. This would be disastrous for health. As Richard Wilkinson has put it, 'In Britain, as in many other countries, the scale of the excess mortality associated with lower social status dwarfs almost every other health problem'.[81] The latest study from Northern England shows that this problem has increased further between 1981 and 1991.[82] In the next round of reforms, unlike in 1911, it is imperative that society is not forced once again up the wrong path.

References

1.Whitehead M. *Inequalities in Health: The Health Divide*. London, Penguin, 1992.
2.Pappas G, Queen S, Hadden W, Fisher G. The increasing disparity in mortality between socioeconomic groups in the United States, 1960 and 1986. *New England Journal of Medicine* 1993; 329:103-109.
3.Angell M. Privilege and health - what is the connection? *New England Journal of Medicine* 1993; 329:126-127.
4.Nissel M. *People Count: a history of the General Register Office*. London, HMSO, 1987.
5.Boston G F P. *Occupation, Industry, Social Class and Socio-Economic Group, 1911-1984*. London, OPCS, 1984.
6.OPCS. *Mortality Statistics: serial tables, England and Wales*. Series DH1, no. 25. London, HMSO, 1992.
7.Department of Health and Social Security. *Inequalities in Health: report of a research working group*. London, DHSS, 1980.
8.OPCS. *Occupational Mortality: decennial supplement 1979-1980, 1982-1983*. London, HMSO, 1986.
9.*Financial statement and budget report, 1979-1980*. London, HMSO, 1979.
10.Haberman M A, Bloomfield D S F. Social class differentials in mortality in Great Britain around 1981. *Journal of the Institute of Actuaries*. 1988; 115:495-517.
11.Whitehead M. Deaths foretold. *The Guardian*, 7 December 1988.
12.Scott-Samuel A, Blackburn P. Crossing the health divide - mortality attributable to social inequality in Great Britain. *Health Promotion* 1988; 2:243-245.
13.Townsend P. Quoted in Whitehead M. *Inequalities in Health: The Health Divide*. London, Penguin, 1992, p231.
14.Blane D, Davey Smith G, Bartley M. Social class differences in years of potential life lost: size, trends, and principal causes. *British Medical Journal*, 1990; 301:429-432.
15.Blaxter M. Evidence on inequality in health from a national survey. *Lancet* 1987; 2:30-33.
16.Goldblatt P. Mortality and alternative social classifications. In P Goldblatt (ed), *Longitudinal Study 1971-81: mortality and social organisation*. OPCS

LS series no 6. London, HMSO, 1990.
17. Pamuk E R. Social class inequality in mortality from 1921-1972 in England and Wales. *Population Studies* 1985; 39:17-31.
18. Goldblatt P. Social class mortality differences. In: N M Mascie-Taylor (ed), *Bio-social Aspects of Social Class*. Oxford, Oxford University Press, 1990.
19. OPCS. *General Household Survey for 1989*, no 20. London, HMSO, 1991.
20. Wilkinson R G. Socio-economic differences in mortality: interpreting the data on their size and trends. In: R G Wilkinson (ed), *Class and Health: research and longitudinal data*. Tavistock, 1986.
21. Goldblatt P. Mortality by social class, 1971-85. *Population Trends* 1989; 56:6-15.
22. Marmot M G, Shipley M J, Rose G. Inequalities in death - specific explanations of a general pattern? *Lancet* 1984; 1:1003-1006.
23. Simpson O. Trends in major risk factors: cigarette smoking. *Postgraduate Medical Journal* 1984; 60:20-25.
24. Berkman L F, Breslow L. *Health and Ways of Living: the Alameda County Study*. Oxford, Oxford University Press, 1983.
25. Registrar General. *The Story of the General Register Office and its Origins from 1536 to 1937*. London, HMSO, 1937.
26. Glass D V. *Numbering the people*. Farnborough, Saxon House, 1973.
27. Malthus T R. *An Essay on the Principle of Population as It Affects the Future Improvement of Society, with Remarks on the Speculations of Mr Godwin, M Concordet and Other Writers*. 1798.
28. Engels F. *The Condition of the Working Class in England*. Oxford, Oxford University Press, 1993.
29. Spencer H. Structure, *Function and Evolution*. London, Nelson, 1971.
30. McKeown T, Lowe C R. *An Introduction to Social Medicine*. London, Blackwell 1974.
31. Muir Gray J A. *Man against Disease. Preventive Medicine*. Oxford, Oxford University Press, 1979.
32. Logan W P D. Mortality in England and Wales from 1848-1947. *Population Studies*, 1950-1951, 4.
33. George H. *Progress and Poverty*. New York, Robert Schalkenbach Foundation, 1979.
34. Simon J. *English Sanitary Conditions* (2nd edition). London, Smith, Elder and Co, 1897.
35. *Royal Commission on the Poor Laws and Relief of Distress*. Report. London, HMSO, 1909.
36. *Royal Commission on the Poor Laws and Relief of Distress*. Minority Report.

London, HMSO, 1909.

37.Douglas R. *Land, People and Politics. A history of the land question in the United Kingdom, 1878-1952.* London, Allison and Busby, 1976, p135.

38.Kay J A, King M A. *The British Tax System* (2nd edition). Oxford, Oxford University Press, 1980.

39.Webb B, Webb S. *History of Trade Unionism,* (revised edition). London, Longmans, 1920, p376.

40.Anon, Land Reform in Politics. *Land and Liberty,* London, February and March, 1964.

41.Ministry of Health. *Consultative Council on Medical and Allied Services. Interim Report on the Future Provision of Medical and Allied Services.* London, HMSO, 1920.

42.Pater J E. *The Making of the National Health Service.* London. King Edward's Hospital Fund for London, 1981, p19.

43.Editorial. The end of the beginning, *Lancet* 1942; 2:623-624.

44.Great Britain, Parliament. *Social Insurance and Allied Services: Report.* London, HMSO, 1942. Cmd. 6404.

45.Ministry of Health and Department of Health for Scotland. *A National Health Service.* London, HMSO, 1944. Cmd 6502.

46.Pater J E. *The Making of the National Health Service.* London, King Edward's Hospital Fund for London. 1981, p115.

47.*Royal Commission on the Distribution of Income and Wealth.* Report no 7. London, HMSO, 1979. Cmd 7595.

48.Haralambos M, Holborn M. *Sociology: Themes and Perspectives.* London, Unwin Hyman, 1990, p51.

49.Townsend P, Whitehead M, Davidson N. *Inequalities in Health.* London, Penguin, 1992, pp1-27.

50.Norton-Taylor R. *Whose Land is it Anyway?* Wellingborough, Turnstone Press, 1982, p24.

51.Public Health Alliance, Scotland. *Housing and Health in Scotland,* 1993.

52.Niner P. *Housing needs in the 1990's.* London: National Housing Forum, 1989.

53.Scottish Homes. *Scottish Housing Condition Survey 1991.* A Report to the Scottish Office and Scottish Homes Board. Preliminary findings. Edinburgh: Scottish Homes, 1993.

54.Platt S D, Martin C J, Hunt S M, Lewis C W. Damp housing, mould growth and symptomatic health state. *British Medical Journal* 1989; 298:1673-78.

55.National Economic Development Office. *Cyclical fluctuations in the UK economy.* Discussion Paper 3. NEDO, 1976, p4.

56.Harrison F. *The Power in the Land*. London: Shepheard-Walwyn (Publishers) Ltd, 1983.
57.Stanley J. The Government and the Construction Industry. Memo by the Minister for Housing and Construction. London, National Economic Development Corporation (82) 5, mimeo.
58.Howarth V. *A survey of families in bed and breakfast hotels: report to the governors of the Thomas Coram Foundation for Children*. London: Thomas Coram Foundation, 1987.
59.Civic Trust. *Urban Wasteland*. London, 1977.
60.*The Building Societies Gazette*, n.d. June, 1981, pp 816-17.
61.Tighe C, Tucker J. Rent rises undermine spirit of enterprise. *Sunday Times*, 5.7.81.
62.Independent Radio News. London, 30.11.80, transcript, p6.
63.Rona R J, Swan A V, Altman D G. Social factors and height of primary school children in England and Scotland. *Journal of Epidemiology and Community Health* 1978; 32:147-54.
64.Chinnock A, Keegan T, Fox P T, Elston M D. Associations between growth patterns, social factors, morbidity and developmental delay in a longitudinal survey of pre-school children. In: J Borns (ed.) *Human Growth and Development*. London: Plenum, 1984.
65.Moser K A, Goldblatt P O, Fox A J, Jones D R. Unemployment and mortality: comparison of the 1971 and 1981 longitudinal study census samples. *British Medical Journal* 1987; 294:86-90.
66.Crombie I K, Kenicer M B, Smith W C S, Tunstall-Pedoe H D. Unemployment, socioenvironmental factors, and coronary heart disease in Scotland. *British Heart Journal* 1989; 61:172-77.
67.Smith R. "What's the point. I'm no use to anybody": the psychological consequences of unemployment. *British Medical Journal* 1985; 291:1338-41.
68.Warr P. Job loss, unemployment and psychological well being. In: V L Allen, E van de Vliert (eds). *Role transitions*. New York, Plenum, 1984.
69.Banks M H, Jackson P R. Unemployment and risk of minor psychiatric disorder in young people: cross sectional and longitudinal evidence. *Psychological Medicine* 1982; 12:789-798.
70.Brenner M H. *Mental Illness and the Economy*. Cambridge, Mass., Harvard University Press, 1973.
71.George H. *The Crime of Poverty*. London: Henry George Foundation of Great Britain, 1938.
72.Kilmarnock. House of Lords *Hansard*. 1987; 1st April: Col 645.

73.Churchill W S. *The People's Rights*. London: Jonathan Cape, 1970.
74.Douglas R. *Land, People and Politics*. London; Allison and Busby, 1976.
75.Bottomley A G. Reynolds News, 28th February 1954.76.Galbraith J K. The good society considered: the economic dimension. *Journal of Law and Society*, in press. Also reported in *The Guardian*, 26th January, 1994.
77.Galbraith J K. *Economics in Perspective. A Critical History*. Boston: Houghton Mifflin Company, 1987.
78.Marx K. *Capital*. London, Lawrence and Wishart, 1962.
79.Galbraith J K. *The Affluent Society*, 4th edition. Penguin; 1991, p44.
80.Friedman M. Comment during debate of the American Education League. Quoted in *Human Events*, 18.11.78, p.14.
81.Wilkinson R G. Divided we fall. The poor pay the price of increased social inequality with their health. *British Medical Journal* 1994; 308:1113-1114.
82.Phillimore P, Beattie A, Townsend P. Widening inequality of health in northern England, 1981-91. *British Medical Journal* 1994; 308:1125-1128.

Public Finance and the Co-operative Society

Kris Feder

The Single Tax Complex

In graduate school I had the good fortune to study with Professor Ingrid Rima, author of one of the most widely-read texts on the history of economic thought. (Rima, 1986) When I asked to write a term paper on George, she indulged my wish with a word of caution. "Henry George," she gently explained, "is merely a footnote in the history of economic thought."

This took me somewhat by surprise, since I had heard that no economic writer had ever sold more books than had George. I had assumed that there must be some reasonable basis for his popularity, and that the profession would not have overlooked it. True, George never won acceptance within academia during his lifetime, largely by his own doing; he openly doubted the intellectual honesty of the professors, and even suggested that ordinary citizens could study political economy without the guidance of books and teachers. Surely by now, however, emotion will have long since cooled, and scholarship taken its place. Economists will have picked George clean, exploiting whatever useful ideas they can find, while carefully exposing the nature of his errors. Historians of thought will have searched beneath the particulars of personality, religion, class, and language to identify George's lasting contributions—if any there are—to economic science. Evidently, if Rima's evaluation represented the consensus opinion, then economic scholars must have determined that George's theory offered nothing both new and true.

123

I found that Rima's judgment is indeed the majority view of economists, at least in regard to the program of rent taxation for which George is known. It is, though, an opinion of long standing, not one which has finally been reached after decades of searching analysis and controversy. Seventy years ago, the Georgist public finance economist H. G. Brown observed:

> ... the majority ... of those who write our current textbooks on economics and on public finance have long regarded single-taxers as utterly unsound thinkers whose economic philosophy should be by all means clearly and definitely discredited. (Brown, 1924: 164)

Brown held that these authorities "have nevertheless failed to grasp entirely the theory on which support of the single tax is based." Textbook writers had caricatured, or, very often, simply ignored, many of single-taxers' arguments, even while complaining of alleged difficulties in the Georgist program. Brown attributed these attitudes and errors to an affliction which he called the "single tax complex." Textbook writers work hard to avoid meeting the Georgists' reasoning head-on because they reject *a priori* the policy conclusion to which it leads. "Being above all things scientists, they are more interested in showing the non-conformity of the policy to their intuitive ethics than they are in exhibiting its probable consequences!" (182)

Several later writers sympathetic to George have expressed similar views of the mainstream attitude. In 1941, George Geiger wrote that the vague idea of "progress and poverty" had become "commonplace," but that George's emphasis on the land question had found no acceptance. Henry George is "the forgotten man." The "neglectful contempt" for his philosophy is "one of the most curious anomalies of the entire literature of social reform." Geiger found the reasons to be unsatisfactory: the land question is out of date; the single tax was to be a "panacea"; single taxers are "crackpots." George believed in God, and in classical economics. Mostly, however, George "is simply outside their universe of discourse." (Geiger, 1941: 87-88)

Geiger hinted that the shelving of the land question may turn out to be a mistake with far-reaching consequences. He was moderately heartened, however, to observe an increasing recognition of the usefulness of what, in the literature, was called Land Value Taxation (LVT) in "town and regional planning." (103, 88)

Three decades later, George's place in history had little changed, and Stuart Bruchey could write of the "twice forgotten man." Yet Bruchey was confident that George was winning partial acceptance. He explained that although George's "system" of economics, constructed in defence of his key principle, had failed, its "kernel" survives. "Georgist principles have clearly entered the mainstream of modern thought." For example, experts on real estate taxation have come to agree that land value taxation "has no harmful effect of any sort on housing quality," despite doubts concerning equity and yield. Also, LVT is recommended for land-rich, capital-poor countries as a means of stimulating capital formation and discouraging underuse of land. (Bruchey, 1972: 119)

Economics of Henry George: The Kernel
Insofar as Georgist principles have "entered the mainstream," they have done so largely anonymously. It is well, therefore, to review the "kernel" of the forgotten theory. George traces the problem of "progress and poverty" to the institution of private property in land. The remedy is "to make land common property" (George, 1879: 326) by the simple fiscal device of collecting land rent in taxation, leaving exclusive, exchangeable land titles undisturbed. Rent should then be distributed fairly among individuals through the reduction or elimination of other taxes, government provision of public goods, and perhaps direct per capita payments.

> ... to take for public purposes the increasing values that attach to land with social growth ... (is) the only means by which it is possible in an advanced civilization to combine the security of possession that is necessary to improvement with the equality of natural opportunity that is the most important of all natural rights. (George, 1879: 434)

If rent were taxed, argued George, both production and distribution would be improved. Production would be stimulated by the removal of taxes which burden production and exchange, as well as by the rent tax itself.

Rent is the opportunity cost of land occupancy. It measures, not the intensity with which land is actually used, but the annual amount which others in the market would be willing to pay for the use of that land. A tax

126 A Philosophy for a Fair Society

on either the rent or the capitalized value of land does not create any incentive to use land less intensively, since the owner cannot thereby reduce his payment. This means that there is no decrease in the market supply of land, no increase in tenants' willingness to pay for the marginal unit of land, and, therefore, no change in the equilibrium quantity or (demand) price of land. The tax cannot even be shifted to future buyers of land, since it is capitalized; the market price of a site falls by the present value of future taxes. The tax is borne by present landowners.

Moreover, the tax is neutral; it generates zero excess burden. This advantage is shared by few other significant sources of government revenue. The greater the revenue raised from a tax on rent, the smaller the revenues required from inefficient taxes on production and exchange. To the extent that taxes on productive activity inhibit production, their removal will stimulate it. George shared the concerns of modern "supply side" economists: "Today taxation operates upon energy, and industry, and skill, and thrift, like a fine upon those qualities." (434)

George further argued that the taxation of land values would discourage land speculation, so that "land now withheld from use would be open to improvement." (434) Distribution would become less unequal as rents are diverted from private to public uses, while "wages would rise to the fair earnings of labor." (436) Initially, land rents would fall as speculators deserted the land market. In the long run, the increase in production "would lead to an increase in the value of land—a new surplus which society might take for general purposes." (432)

George appeals to Lockean principles of freedom and equality to show that his remedy accords with justice. Both efficiency and equity require that individuals have private property rights in themselves and in what their effort (labor and saving) produce, so they should be entitled to receive their full wages and interest, untaxed. However, in order to produce anything, individuals must have access to economic land, which encompasses natural resources, location with respect to other natural and community-created resources, and pure space itself—standing-room. Efficiency and justice also, therefore, require that all individuals of all generations have access to land. Land is not produced by individuals, George observes, and therefore cannot rightfully be owned by individuals. Society should, through the agency of representative government, possess the land in common.

In this, George expresses an ancient conviction. What is new is the recognition that there exists a practical way to share land both equitably and efficiently in a modern monetary economy. Obviously, land should not be physically divided and distributed equally, as perhaps it can in the simplest agrarian society. Nor should most land be treated as commons in the sense of unlimited public access; exclusive rights to the use of land are essential. What George shows is that society need not alienate land to individual ownership in fee simple in order to preserve productive incentives.

> The value of land expresses in exact and tangible form the right of the community to land held by an individual; and rent expresses the exact amount which the individual should pay to the community to satisfy the equal rights of all other members of the community. (344)

In fact, George held that absolute ownership of land interferes with its efficient use. Land value taxation is not merely neutral, but better than neutral: it removes impediments to efficient intertemporal and inter-generational use of land that are inherent in the system of absolute private property in land. LVT would break up land monopoly and deter land speculation, both of which cause misallocation of resources. Speculation not only misallocates land; in conjunction with an elastic credit system, it is the major underlying cause of industrial depressions.

George saw the importance of scale economies, externalities and government services in giving value to certain lands. He recognized that urban site values were rapidly overtaking agricultural land values in relative importance, and focused analytical attention on the processes and problems of urban economies.

George supposed that a single tax on land values would always be sufficient for the legitimate needs of government. As progress goes on, individuals become more interdependent economically. However, these activities of society and government give increased value to land, increasing the tax base. (George, 1879. 436)

To George, the tax on rent was key to reconciling the apparent conflict between efficiency and equity. He argued that inequality in land ownership, once established, tends to produce further inequality, ultimately leading to the stagnation and decline of society. Efficient and stable operation of an economy cannot be sustained if principles of equity and freedom are ignored. "In justice is the highest and truest expediency." (367)

Is Anything New and True in Georgist Economics

Is there truth to Brown's diagnosis of a "single tax complex"? Or are there definitive reasons to dismiss George's emphasis on the land question, and to reject his specific tax proposal? Are economists right to relegate George to a "footnote"?

Many economists now admit that LVT has certain advantages over property and other taxes. Milton Friedman once described it as "the least bad tax." (Human Events, Nov. 18, 1978) However, the point is not much advertised. The case for LVT is seen as a minor issue of local tax reform. The full reach of Georgist thought goes unrecognized. Land has apparently lost its special analytical status in economic theory. (Skouras, 1980) Few economists have more than a cursory familiarity with the ideas of Henry George, or of his twentieth century advocates.

> The economists have never seriously attacked the theoretical validity of the single tax program. In the main, in fact, they have come nearer to ignoring than to condemning. (Davenport, 1910: 279)

The words of H. J. Davenport are less true today than they were in 1910—but not very much less. If Georgist economics has been defeated, it is by ignorance, not by argument or evidence.

Meantime, however, a rich and varied Georgist research program is underway. The agenda touches virtually every sub-discipline. Some questions pertain to a spatial, urban economy with externalities and public services. Some pertain to a dynamic economy with money and credit, and with imperfections in land, capital, or other markets. Some focus on savings, capital formation, and growth; others on the vagaries of the business cycle. Yet others refer to issues of public choice, administrative practice and bureaucratic incentives; to questions of population, environment, and sustainable development; even to the grand issues of justice, political stability, and international cooperation.

The time may well be right for a resurgence of interest in Georgist economics, much as Bruchey suggested twenty years ago. It is my belief that George's central economic principle is valid and profound—and that the reasons to pay attention to it are gathering power and urgency.

In the remainder of this section, I discuss the standard reasons offered for rejecting the proposal set forth in *Progress and Poverty*. It is, of course, impossible here to weigh all the arguments against George, or even all the important ones. Instead, I simply list some of them to give the flavor, and focus attention on a few central ones. Two, in particular, appear to be plausible and persistent: first, the judgement that switching to land value taxation is unfair to innocent landowners; and second, the estimate that land rent is an insignificant and declining share of income.

In the second section of this study, I indicate some of the directions, unfamiliar to most economists, in which the Georgist tradition has developed.

In the final section, I conclude that what George offers is not a simplistic panacea, but a paradigm—a conceptual structure built on simple principles, to be sure, but principles which interact in complex ways. As a number of authors have argued, the Georgist paradigm promises to forge a "synthesis" between the "thesis" of capitalism and the "antithesis" of socialism—thereby resolving the tension between the twin social goals of efficiency and equity.

Moreover, the accelerating environmental crisis is the catalyst which makes Georgism an obvious alternative. In the past, George's critics pointed to rising relative wages and falling materials prices as evidence that land is no longer an important factor of production. Yet public concern about resource depletion is deepening. The apparent gains in the efficiency of materials use have come at the cost of drastic increases in the volume and toxicity of wastes spilled into air and water—both also vital *land* resources, the use of which has traditionally been unpriced. Sadly, these frontiers of free land are closing.

We cannot continue to behave as though environmental resources were limitless and valueless. As the global commons grow scarce, and as international political arrangements are negotiated to ration their use, we are faced anew with the question of how to allocate economic land efficiently while distributing its rent equitably.

In conclusion, I shall suggest that most of the tired and tattered old controversies about the "Single Tax panacea" can be put behind us, and that a tantalizing array of new or, at least, neglected research questions awaits pursuit.

2

The Case Against Land Rent Taxation

Robert Heilbroner

Probably the most widely read history of economic thought is Robert Heilbroner's *The Worldly Philosophers*, first published in 1953. It has done as much as any other book to form the opinion of Henry George held by economists, social scientists, and the educated public today.

Unfortunately, Heilbroner shows advanced symptoms of that affliction of textbook writers diagnosed by H. G. Brown, the "single tax complex." George is depicted as a good-hearted but simple-minded amateur, driven by childish enthusiasm and self-assurance, who gravely underestimated the difficulty of the world's economic problems. Heilbroner does not waste space explaining George's actual theory. He devotes seven pages to colorful (and partly fanciful) biography; about a page to George's economics. "We need not spell out the whole emotionally charged argument," he says. (Heilbroner, 1986: 188)

What explanation he does provide distorts George's views unrecognizably. Heilbroner fails both to convey the basic principles of George's economics, and to suggest the richness of George's philosophy as a whole. Moreover, even in the "completely revised" sixth edition of 1986, there is no hint of the fact that later writers have formalized and vastly extended the Georgist approach.

"The argument was not too clearly delineated," Heilbroner writes. (188) "George's mechanical diagnosis is superficial and faulty." (189) Actually, George's argument was painstakingly delineated over the course of several hundred pages, and while it may be faulty, superficial it surely is not.

More damaging, however, is the fact that Heilbroner ascribes to him a patently absurd position—the "equation of rent with sin." (189) Henry George, we are told, wanted to "abolish" rent! In fact, of course, George believed that rent is a social surplus which would steadily grow as progress goes on; what he wanted was to have rent collected publicly rather than privately.

Heilbroner pauses somewhat longer to give a few of the standard arguments against the single tax. He refers, for example, to George's treatment of land speculation, but only to reject his explanation of the business cycle as a far-fetched exaggeration. "Land speculations can be troublesome," he declares, "but severe depressions have taken place in countries where land values were anything but inflated." (189) No evidence or reference is offered. (The innocent reader presumes that economists have by now achieved consensus as to the true cause of depressions.)

"The single tax," chuckles Heilbroner, "in abolishing rent ... would be— there is no other word—the ultimate panacea." (188-189) The reader is led to infer that no trained economist today is seriously interested in George. Just as Brown complained seventy years ago—and Geiger, fifty-three, and Bruchey, twenty-four—students have been forewarned that George was a crackpot, and that it is not worthwhile to look further in his direction.

It is no surprise that Heilbroner misses the irony of his next words:

> But something else was going on in the underworld, something more important than Henry George's fulminations against rent .... A new and vigorous spirit was sweeping England and the Continent and even the United States .... The age of imperialism had begun, and the mapmakers were busy changing the colors that denoted ownership of the darker continents. (191-192)

Joseph Schumpeter

In his *History of Economic Analysis*, Schumpeter makes clear that he has no use for the single tax "panacea." (Schumpeter, 1954: 865) He indicates that he has "compunctions about the analytic value of the proposition: God gave the earth in common to all men." (458) He disparages one writer (Oppenheimer) for "his Henry-George attitude toward private property in land." (854) Despite this, Schumpeter shows relatively few symptoms of the single tax complex. He allows that George's program benefits from good analysis, insofar as it causes minimum disruption of economic efficiency. He recognizes George as "a very orthodox economist" except with regard to the "Single Tax." (865) His specific criticisms are rather well-aimed, and worth recalling.

Schumpeter imputes to George the thesis that the existence of private property in land "reduces, of necessity, total real wages" (458), and is the reason why land is a scarce factor at all (854 note). In this, he has identified what may be the key argument of *Progress and Poverty* - an argument which, indeed, may not be quite strong enough to support the weight it carries.

The suggestion implicit in Schumpeter's remark is that to transfer land rent from private to public hands would not, of itself, affect wages. Against this it may by noted that, by financing an ever-growing public sector, the single tax would, if not raise wages, at least raise real *incomes*, insofar as workers (like other citizens) are enabled to consume progressively more government-financed goods and services. Surely, too, to collect land rent in lieu of taxes on labor and products will obviously and directly raise after-tax real wages, in the short run at least. But George does not rely on this argument. In fact, he says in another place that under the existing land tenure system, a decrease in taxes made possible by greater economy in government will, in the long run, benefit landowners, not laborers. (301)

George's primary defense of the assertion that his tax plan will raise wages is the claim that LVT will curb land speculation, thereby raising the margin of production, which determines the equilibrium level of wages:

> Labor and capital would thus not merely gain what is now taken from them in taxation, but would gain by the positive decline in rent caused by the decrease in speculative land values. (George, 1879: 442)

Whatever be the truth to this, there is some internal difficulty in George's view. On the one hand, he vehemently rejects Malthusianism, arguing that land is so plentiful that the Earth could comfortably support a population many times larger than that which prevailed in 1879. This seems to imply that the present population could comfortably occupy just a small fraction of the space available. Yet on the other hand, George argues that land speculators, by withholding some land from use, collectively wield tremendous power to exploit labor and capital. The evident contradiction is perhaps not entirely eliminated by supposing that speculation not only reduces the amount of land in use, but also diminishes the efficiency with which that land is used.

Schumpeter finds a second flaw in the logic of *Progress and Poverty*. This is the "untenable theory that the phenomenon of poverty is entirely due to the absorption of all surpluses by the rent of land." There may be a suggestion here of the familiar argument that land rent is merely one surplus among many, which I discuss below. Schumpeter may also be referring specifically to George's argument that all the gains from population growth and technological advance ultimately go to the increase of rent. Although other classical economists are equally to blame for holding an all-devouring rent thesis, this does not excuse George; in particular, he might have seen that technological change may be land-saving instead of labor-saving, particularly as land becomes scarcer relative to labor. He might also have seen that as technical progress goes on, access to education becomes an increasingly important factor in income distribution.

It is one thing to argue that the elaborate classical system which George constructed to support his central thesis contains errors. It is quite another thing to show that the central thesis is unsupportable. About this, Schumpeter has little to say. Despite his reservations, he concludes with the enigmatic but not unsympathetic comment that George's proposal is "not *economically* unsound, except in that it involves an unwarranted optimism concerning the yield of such a tax." (865, italics added)

Is the reader to infer that the principle of rent taxation is economically sound, except that it is inadequate as a single tax? Is the tax perhaps *ethically* or *politically* unsound? Whatever be the intent of Schumpeter's negatively phrased affirmation, his pessimism concerning yield, which he shares with Heilbroner, is unfair and probably unwarranted: unfair, because government budgets were far smaller a century ago—George's contemporary critics feared that the yield of the single tax would be excessive, giving undue power to government. Unwarranted, because there are good reasons to suppose that the yield of a single tax on the full rent of land would be far larger than his critics today suppose, as I shall indicate below.

Arguments Against Rent Taxation

Opponents of the Georgist program have offered numerous additional counterarguments. Many of those which recur frequently are either unsound or irrelevant. A few have value and warrant careful attention, though none vitiates the fundamental Georgist insight.

It is argued, for example:

• that a switch to heavy LVT is unfair to vested interests;

• that the tax would not reach most of those who have, in the past, benefited from private property in land;

• that land rent is merely one among many surpluses;

• that rent is not a surplus at all, but a reward for putting land to its best use;

• that land values sometimes fall;

• that land taxation will not raise real wages;

• that many low- and middle-income households own land;

• that LVT will throw the urban poor out of their homes;

• that LVT will bankrupt small farmers;

• that LVT puts government in the business of land management;

• that the value of land cannot be distinguished from that of capital improvements;

• that "land" denotes no meaningful, distinct economic entity;

• that the supply of land is not perfectly inelastic as the theory allegedly requires, since more land can be produced—or, since land can be turned from one use to another;

• that land value taxation distorts intertemporal resource allocation by hastening development;

• that land speculation is efficient, and should be encouraged;

• that the tax will worsen speculation, or have no effect upon it;

• that the tax will cause severe cash flow problems for owners of appreciating land;

• that land speculation is not a cause, or the primary cause, of business cycles;

• that LVT induces land abandonment;

• that LVT will cause overbuilding, further congesting urban areas and destroying open land;

• that rent taxation discourages conservation, and induces ecologically

unsound exploitation of resources;
* that the single tax gives inordinate power to government, and leads inevitably to institutionalized corruption; or,
* that land rent constitutes an insignificant share of national income, so the tax would raise little revenue and would have a barely noticeable effect on economic behavior.

Textbooks continue to repeat old errors. Most textbook discussions of George confine their analytical comments to a cursory exposition of the inelastic-supply argument for land tax neutrality. Sometimes, the conventional theorem that a tax on rent cannot be shifted is denied, on the ground that a rise in rent will bring a large supply of land to market, or even stimulate production of more land.

There is also usually a mention of distributive impact; the program is generally felt to be unfair. Income and other taxes are promoted as capturing alternative sources of surplus. These are generally pushed on grounds of equity and revenue adequacy. Income taxes share few of the efficiency properties claimed for rent taxation. On the other hand, none of these writers has fully come to terms with the Georgist view of economic justice—this despite evidence that, because of wholesale tax (and subsidy) shifting, our ambitious and costly redistributive programs have had little sustained effect upon the distribution of disposable income. (Holcombe, 1987: 286-288)

It is not my intent to confront most of these objections. I discuss two of the more prevalent ones below, before going on to discuss further developments in Georgist economics. My aim is to show that the case for using rent as a source of government revenue is far wider and richer than is commonly realized. The various superneutrality arguments are virtually unknown. Also, economists have neither understood nor challenged the Georgist view of the abundant revenue potential of rent taxation.

Problems of Transition to a Georgist World
There is one objection which occurs even to those who are sympathetic to George's vision of economic justice and who understand the efficiency arguments. This is the objection that, even if a Georgist world is in principle to be preferred to our own, for an established economy/polity to undertake a transition to heavy or exclusive reliance on rent taxation would cause

unconscionable harm. It would unfairly penalize the wrong individuals, violate vested interests, and shake public faith in government. The essence of this complaint is that it is not fair to change the rules in the middle of the game. Georgist tax reform would result in windfall losses to some individuals (and gains to others).

Since LVT cannot be shifted, the entire burden of the program falls on the backs of those individuals who happen to own land at the time the tax is announced. The tax neutrality/nonshiftability argument, usually seen as the first pillar of LVT theory, thus becomes a potent political and ethical argument against it. Voters accept income taxes, sales taxes and the rest precisely *because* they are shifted around, their burdens diffused widely and in imperceptible ways.

Georgists have several responses, none of which convinces everyone.

They hold that rule changes consequent upon public resolve to correct a newly recognized injustice tend to promote, rather than erode, public faith in government. Moreover, land is different. Georgists point out that in common law, real estate ("regal estate") is the property of the State, and that private rights to land are conditional on the use being consistent with the public interest. We accept zoning as well as some degree of land value taxation, for example, as well as the principle of eminent domain, which, where it is applied, can be far more disruptive of vested interests that would be a well-orchestrated transition to a regime based on resource rent taxation.

Anyhow, legislatures and courts make rule changes every day. Some cause significant redistribution of welfare, as when tax codes are overhauled. Taken too literally, the vested rights protest becomes an absurd defense of the *status quo*. Defenders respond, of course, that to "make land common property" by taxing rent is an exceedingly drastic step. (One wonders what advice these conservative writers might have offered to the countries of the former Soviet Union and Eastern Europe.) George observed that slavery was rightly abolished with no compensation paid to slave owners. Defenders of vested interests recall the Civil War.

Some land taxers have regretted George's blunt words, emphasizing that their purpose, however radical, is achieved by a simple, gradual, unobtrusive adjustment of the rates of familiar taxes.

Perhaps the argument most convincing to economists is that, if Georgists are right, the proposed regime change constitutes a potential Pareto-superior move. Depending on transaction costs, it may be possible to arrange a compensation system during the transitional period, paying net losers out of the winnings of the net gainers. This may not be as difficult as it sounds. A gradual, rather than abrupt, shift to heavier land taxation provides a significant degree of compensation automatically, since the present value of future taxes, capitalized into lower current land prices, is smaller, the longer the reform is postponed. It also allows investors to adjust their plans to a new set of rules. Moreover, since an increase in the LVT rate would be accompanied by a decrease in other taxes, there would be very few individuals (in the United States at least) who, on balance, stood to suffer a net loss of appreciable magnitude. Those other taxes had been shifted at least partly to land. Even individuals who lose in the short run are likely to find themselves better off in the long run than they would have been without the reform.

A related argument against the Georgist plan is that a rent tax would fall only on current landowners, many of whom are recent buyers; it wholly exempts past landowners—who have already realized their unearned gains. The injustice to which George objects, if it is an injustice at all, is a regrettable but immutable fact of history. As Heilbroner observed:

> A vast body of rents goes to small landholders, farmers, homeowners, modest citizens. ... Rents are not frozen in archaic feudal patterns, but constantly pass from hand to hand as land is bought and sold, appraised and reappraised. (Heilbroner, 1986: 190)

George's reply to this line of argument was that the purpose of his reform, like any other, was intended to correct, not past, but present and future injustice. (The complaint carries more force in the United States than in some other places, such as where the legacy of European colonialism includes the *latifundia* [great estates] of a powerful aristocracy—much like those which, George reminds us, weakened the Roman Empire.)

The real issue is whether the efficiency and equity benefits of the proposed reform would be sufficiently large to justify the necessary expenditure of political will and disruption of expectations. The first constructive task, as Brown observed, is to predict the likely effects of the Georgist plan once it is in place. If they are desirable, the reasonable next step is to search for the most satisfactory way to achieve the transition.

One obvious place to begin is with the vast resources not yet subject to private property. Raise logging and grazing fees on federal lands to market levels—or higher, to reflect the environmental costs of these activities. Charge polluters for permission to foul the air, water, and soil; negotiate international agreements to allow fair, efficient, and sustainable use of the global commons. At the level of local politics, one place to start is by gradual reform of the real estate tax, just as cities in Pennsylvania and New York have done.

All these are already on the agenda in the United States. Ironically, public opinion seems in some respects to be bending unwittingly in George's direction.

One Surplus Among Many

A second persistent argument against the Georgist proposal is that, while land rent is surplus, there are many other important sources of surplus (or unearned income) as well. This view, only suggested by Schumpeter, is central to Heilbroner's critique:

> ... (L)andlords are not the only passive beneficiaries of the growth of society. The stockholder in an expanding company, the workman whose productivity is enhanced by technical progress, the consumer whose real income rises as the nation prospers, all these are also beneficiaries of communal advancement. The unearned gains that accrue to a well-situated landlord are enjoyed in different forms by all of us. (Heilbroner, 1986: 189)

"Neo-Georgist" Kenneth Boulding agreed that rent taxation is equitable as well as efficient, and that the tax system is the ideal instrument with which to socialize rent. However, he emphasized that land rent is only one of several varieties of taxable surplus; the "single tax" alone is insufficient to capture it all. (Boulding,1982: 8) Boulding suggested that graduated income taxes are appropriate to achieve the redistribution George desired.

Perhaps the movement that undermined George's influence more than any other was the rise of the progressive income tax, most of which took place after the publication of *Progress and Poverty*. In the opinion of most economists and men of affairs, this represented a method of redistribution, even the capture of economic surplus, which was more general than any land tax. (17)

Even if they reach some surplus, however, income taxes tap both earned and unearned income indiscriminately; they share few of the efficiency properties claimed for land value taxation. Moreover, since they are easily shifted, there is no assurance that income taxes affect the distribution of welfare as anticipated. George wrote that the goal of the progressive income tax—a more equal distribution—is worthy, but that its enforcement encourages bribery and evasion, and involves needless restriction of freedom. Worse, "Just in proportion as the tax accomplishes its effect, there is a lessening in the incentive to accumulate wealth, which is one of the strong forces of industrial progress." (George, 1879: 320)

In any case, Heilbroner's suggested alternative surpluses are suspect. In the first place, the gains received by a "stockholder in an expanding company" are interest and profit, not "surplus"; without such gains, corporations could not attract scarce capital, especially for risky ventures. Whereas a new buyer in the land market merely raises the price of the fixed stock of land, a new buyer in the stock market increases the aggregate of corporate capital.

LVT is not intended to capture entrepreneurial profit, which is a reward for risk and ingenuity. One who acquires land by purchase in a well-informed market and possesses no monopoly power enjoys no "unearned income" in the accepted sense unless there are land gains not foreseen and capitalized in the purchase price. If a certain landowning entrepreneur is able to extract a net income which exceeds the opportunity cost of the land, as measured by the market rent, then that excess is profit; it is not, and should not be, captured by a rent tax.

Ordinary monopoly profits, George knew, are indeed another source of unearned advantage. His preferred solution was either to abolish the entry barrier which produces the monopoly, or, in the case of natural monopoly, to have the activity regulated by government. Either way, there will be nothing left to tax.

In the second place, rent is a surplus only in the sense that land would exist regardless of who received its rent. More to the point, rent is the social opportunity cost of land occupancy. Rent rations scarce land services, which are rival benefits: one person's enjoyment of these general gains interferes with another's. By contrast, the rising real wages and incomes

enjoyed by workers and consumers "as the nation prospers" are clearly
nonrival benefits; one person's enjoyment deprives no other. These widely
shared "surpluses" are a cause, not for alarm, but for celebration.

Heilbroner tells us that George wanted to "abolish rent" because rent has
made some people rich. He was "outraged" at the sometimes "fabulous"
incomes of fortunate landlords. (Heilbroner, 1986: 188) However, George
was not at all opposed to wealth. On the contrary, he wished we could all
be rich; he praised the technical and social advances which promise to make
the wish come true. His book inquires, not why some men are rich, but why,
despite a century of undreamed-of material progress, so many are poor.

3

Developments in Georgist Economics

Incentive Taxation: Neutrality and Superneutrality
Advocates of land value taxation argue that LVT not only is neutral in its effect on efficient resource allocation, but even generates incentives which tend to correct certain types of market imperfections and to promote economic growth.

Wealth and Portfolio Effects. When land is considered solely as a factor of production, then (ignoring income effects) a tax on rent cannot be shifted. If land is considered as an asset in investors' portfolios, however, then the traditional conclusion is modified. As Feldstein and others have shown, wealth and portfolio effects may cause shifting of the tax onto capital. This consideration has implications for income distribution and economic growth.

In his analysis of production and wealth, Henry George contrasted "value from obligation" with "value from production." (George, 1879: 434) The former, which includes land and monopoly privileges, does not constitute wealth from a social viewpoint, since in the aggregate each credit is balanced by a debit. George believed that when ownership of these assets substitutes for ownership of true wealth, production and capital formation suffer.

Today, a variety of models confirm that the existence of private property in land diverts savings away from investment in productive capital. Land value taxation reduces the private equity and increases the public equity in land. Capital is substituted for land in investor portfolios, promoting capital formation and economic growth. Also, wealth and portfolio effects may shift some part of the burden of a land value tax to owners of produced capital (not only capital invested in real estate, but all capital). Significantly, wages may increase as a consequence. (Dwyer, 1982: 369; Nichols, 1970; Skouras, 1977; Feldstein, 1977)

Wealth effects may occur because LVT reduces the stock of private assets. Depending on savings motives and on the disposition of the tax revenue, this may induce households to attempt to buy more of all assets in order to return to their desired level of savings. If the taxing region is large enough, this bids up the prices of both land and capital. More land cannot be produced, but more capital can be, and is. In the long run, therefore, the marginal productivity (and rate of return) of capital falls, while the marginal productivity of land rises; there is some shifting of the land tax onto capital. (The decline in the interest rate raises the capitalized value of land.) There may also be an increase in wages, as the increase of capital raises the marginal productivity of labor. (Nichols, 1970; Feldstein, 1977: 350-353)

Since land and other assets are not necessarily equally risky investments, LVT may be shifted through portfolio effects as well. The tax reduces the ratio of land to capital in private portfolios. If land and capital are not perfect substitutes, investors try to buy land and sell capital in order to return to their desired asset ratio. In the short run, this merely drives up the price of land, again resulting in a shifting of the tax. (Feldstein, 1977: 354-358)

It is important to emphasize that tax shifting through income, wealth, and portfolio effects does not compromise the efficiency of LVT. It reflects no tax "wedge" sending distorted price signals to market participants. Instead, Georgists emphasize that by rerouting savings toward productive investment, the wealth effect of LVT promotes capital formation and economic growth efficiently and even-handedly, without recourse to government spending programs, subsidies, or price manipulation. The argument carries special force in many land-rich, capital-starved developing countries. (Skouras, 1977; Nichols, 1970) Land value taxation is urged as a valuable tool with which to accumulate capital while improving the distribution of wealth.

Land Taxation and Land Speculation. Several "superneutrality" arguments for LVT indicate that the tax actually improves productive efficiency. (Dwyer, 1981) One such argument begins by pointing out that capital markets are inherently imperfect, since they rely on estimates of future values which cannot be known with certainty. Investors face different discount rates. In financial markets, funds are allocated, not necessarily to those who will use them most productively, but to those who have collateral and can borrow at low interest rates. As Mason Gaffney (1973 and elsewhere) has shown, a (small) firm can sometimes be outbid in the land market by a (large) buyer who discounts future returns at a lower rate, even if the low bidder can employ the land more productively. The marginal condition for efficient factor employment is violated. This distortion is greatest for land which is appreciating in value.

LVT improves the efficiency of land allocation by reducing dependence on credit markets. Since it is capitalized into lower land prices, LVT simply substitutes an annual (tax) payment for a lump-sum (land price) payment of equal present value. This replaces the interest cost of landholding with an impartial tax cost, neutralizing the effect of credit discrimination. The result is a tendency for land, especially appreciating land at the fringes of growing cities, to be transferred from speculators to users, and therefore to be used with increased intensity as well as efficiency. (Gaffney, 1973)

LVT systematically discourages inefficient land speculation and underutilization in other ways, as well. While the tax cost is an explicit charge, the interest cost of holding land is borne only implicitly if owners are unencumbered by mortgages. The annual tax may make landowners more keenly aware of the opportunity cost of land. It creates a cash flow problem for owners who irrationally or unknowingly waste opportunities to earn an income from their land. LVT prods them to action, pressing them either to put the land to its best use or to sell it to someone who will.

Suppose a speculator buys land merely to hold, in anticipation of a rise in its value. Figuring that the appreciation rate will be sufficient to at least cover the interest cost of the investment, he deliberately chooses to forego the rents which could be earned in the interim. True, he fails to maximize his gain. Such inefficient land speculation nevertheless occurs for a variety of reasons, among them gambling, inertia, and indecision. Perhaps the speculator has no special expertise at land development, and prefers to invest any available funds in more land, rather than in buildings. Transaction costs may preclude his temporarily leasing the land to a tenant, even if there exist worthwhile interim uses which potentially could earn enough to amortize sunk capital before the land "ripens" to some higher use. (Brown, 1927; Gaffney, 1961)

LVT increases the penalty for inefficient speculation of this sort. The tax is capitalized in land value, which leaves total holding costs for the speculator—interest plus taxes—unchanged. But the higher is the LVT rate, the smaller is the capital gain for which those constant holding costs are incurred. The tax pressures owners to put land to its best use. (Brown, 1927)

Land hoarding can reflect ordinary monopoly power as well as speculation or capital market imperfections. As Henry George observed, since no more land can be produced, its exclusive ownership creates a primary condition of monopoly: the existence of barriers to entry. (Gaffney, 1967; Dwyer, 1981: 65-75) The immobility of land is another source of monopoly power. The idea of location as a barrier to entry—spatial monopoly—has recently received some attention from economists. (Dwyer, 1981: 325) Sufficiently heavy taxation of rents or land values, it is argued, erases the incentive to accumulate land with intent to monopolize.

Georgists have only begun to build the case for George's view that land speculation not only misallocates land, but also contributes to regional macroeconomic instability. (Harrison, 1983) A widespread collapse of speculative land prices often precedes a general economic contraction, as it did in 1928, and as it did recently, for example, in the United States (the "S&L crisis") and in Japan. Georgists claim that general reliance on land value taxation will dampen speculative booms and busts.

Location Value
The Henry George Theorem. The allegedly "unpriced" benefits of local public goods are not unpriced at all. They are not sold, however, by the governments which produce them. They are sold to users by the owners of the lands serviced. They are sold as package deals; to buy or rent a location is to purchase scarce access to all the services accessible from that land parcel, whether you avail yourself of them or not. This is simply to say that competitive land rents reflect, in part, the demand for access to those

benefits. This means that if local government expenditure provides services which people want, then with a sufficiently high tax on land rent, those services can be self-financing.

A family of models developed by urban economists indicates that, under certain rather general conditions, a tax on land rent is (not merely nondistortionary but) necessary for full efficiency in a competitive system of cities. Furthermore, the rent increases generated by the optimal level of public expenditure, supplemented where appropriate by efficient marginal-cost user charges, is exactly sufficient to finance the optimal expenditure. This result has been named the "Henry George Theorem," recalling George's conviction that a single tax on land rent would always be adequate to cover the legitimate expenses of government. (Stiglitz, 1974; Vickrey, 1977)

While all the formal conditions of the Henry George Theorem cannot be assumed to be satisfied in the real world, these models nevertheless carry an important lesson. People "buy" local public services when they buy land. They pay more for land in a district with good schools or good roads than for land in a district with poor schools or poor roads, other things equal. For that matter, they also "buy" a package of privately-created externalities. They pay more to live where crime rates are low than they do to live where they are high, other things equal. When land is privately owned, these benefits are captured by landowners. Rent taxation returns this socially-created value to the public. From this perspective, LVT is not a true tax but, as one writer has put it, a "super user charge." (Rybeck, 1983)

Urban rapid transit systems, for example, require immense capital outlays. The costs rise still higher as cities sprawl and the density of land use declines; local governments have to scramble to provide the necessary subsidies. Raising fares diminishes ridership and forfeits the scale economies which are the rationale for mass transit in the first place. Yet we need more subways, not fewer. Mass transit reduces automobile congestion and pollution, reduces the area of valuable central land which must be devoted to streets and parking lots, and helps low-income central city residents get to jobs. If benefit-cost studies indicate that most mass transit systems do not pay, it may be because they fail to account for the benefits which are captured in land values. The lower are fares, the larger is the rise in land value which a transit system bestows on private owners. Land value taxation intercepts publicly-created windfall gains to landowners, making them available to finance public expenditures without distortionary taxation. With 100 percent rent taxation, efficient marginal cost transit fares maximize government profit.

Urban Problems and the Property Tax. Heavy taxation of buildings coupled with undertaxation of land contributes to a staggering list of urban problems: sprawl, leapfrog development, rising costs of municipal services, urban congestion, vacant lots, abandoned buildings, decaying slums, stagnant central cities, and discriminatory zoning practices.

Cities exist because many kinds of economies can best be exploited when land is used at high densities. High density means low transportation costs, easy communication, and intensive utilization of collective consumption goods. High central land values are the key to private-sector urban renewal.

Building taxes are shifted partly or wholly to land, which dampens the incentive to salvage well-situated land by demolishing worn-out buildings. This perverse incentive is especially powerful because new buildings pay higher property taxes than old. Neighbourhood effects from deterioration of old buildings further exacerbate the depressing influence of building taxes, sometimes causing renewal to be delayed indefinitely. A property owner in a blighted area may simply abandon title rather than incur the expense of demolition to recover the site. Every additional abandonment further depresses land values in the neighbourhood.

As central cities are left to decay, people who can afford to get out scatter across the countryside. Urban sprawl multiplies the cost of municipal services, dissipates economies of density in commerce and industry, increases road mileage without lessening traffic congestion, worsens auto pollution, chews up valuable farmland, ruins open space, and pushes jobs to the suburbs, out of reach of the urban poor.

The prices of horizontal transportation are kept artificially low by the subsidies implicit in toll-free roads, cheap gas, and flat-rate pricing of municipal services. The traditional property tax exaggerates the bias against vertical transportation. While streets and sidewalks are provided at public expense, elevators are taxed. Here is another institutional cause of urban sprawl.

Since the burden of a tax on improvements is greatest where buildings are tallest, the largest declines in land value caused by the property tax are in central cities. Accordingly, the "unshifting" which results from the removal of building taxes gives the largest land value increases to central locations. The urban rent function becomes steeper; the city grows more compact.

In short, the traditional property tax obstructs the operation of the synergistic forces which are the reason for being of cities. Conversion to LVT promises to stimulate development efficiently, even-handedly, and continually, without bureaucratic interference and at no cost to taxpayers. It automatically turns the vicious circle of urban decline into a virtuous circle of renewal, as each renovation and redevelopment enhances the values of neighbouring sites. (Gaffney, 1969; 1989)

Land and Environment

Tax Reform and the Environment. The environmental consequences of heavier land value taxation, especially coupled with lighter taxation of improvements, are overwhelmingly favourable, particularly for the artificial environments of urban areas. As the tax bias against improvements is softened, structures will be built better, yet replaced sooner. A sea of downtown parking lots will give way to new offices, stores, restaurants— and a single parking garage. Valuable urban land will be used intensely, providing more indoor space per person. As urban sprawl is reversed, dependence on the automobile will lessen, reducing air pollution, traffic congestion, commuting times, and auto accidents.

Property tax reform carried out unilaterally by a single locality may, in principle, lead to excessive development there, especially if the resident population is highly mobile. If this were to occur, the obvious solution would be to reduce temporarily the land-to-building tax rate differential, while advertising the benefits of tax reform to neighbouring communities. I know of no evidence that overbuilding has ever occurred in two-rate tax regions; rate differentials could go much higher than they are. Unfortunately, our central cities have far to go before they need to worry about overdevelopment. Much of the concrete clutter in downtown areas today is yesterday's trash, still uncleared. Beneath it, potentially valuable land awaits recovery.

Applied nationally, Georgist tax reform would not cause overbuilding, a concern of many critics (unless buildings were actually taxed *less* than other capital). High density at urban centers means low density elsewhere. With speculation and sprawl curbed, fertile, conveniently situated farmland at the fringes of urban areas would be preserved. It would be easier to move around within the city, and easier for city residents to travel to rural areas. Also, insofar as high land taxes are capitalized into low land prices, tax reform makes it easier to acquire land for parks, playgrounds, landscaping, bicycle paths, and the like. Local governments will be rewarded for setting aside open space by the resulting increases in neighbourhood land values and, therefore, tax revenues. (Dywer, 1981: 225) In principle, expenditure on parks should proceed to the point at which the marginal dollar of annual park expenditure (including the foregone rent of park land) generates just one dollar of increase in aggregate annual rent.

LVT and Depletable Resources. It has sometimes been argued that the non-shiftability of taxes on pure site rent does not extend directly to taxes on ownership of depletable resources; annual taxation of mines, for example, would encourage premature extraction. Gaffney has answered that mineral extraction or soil depletion amounts to "the liquidation or amortization of a fund, comparable to sale of title to part of the land itself." (Gaffney, 1964-65: 540) Georgist principles call for a severance tax "equal to the discounted value of the most remote future liquidation receipt"; this amount "is part of land rent." (556) In conjunction with an annual tax on the value remaining in the ground, such a charge is neutral with respect to the optimal rate of extraction. (Gaffney, 1967: 557).

LVT and Nonexclusive Resources. Effluent taxes charged to polluters are assessments for the rent of environmental resources. A system of tradeable emissions permits is rent taxation too, if the permits are sold by government in a competitive auction. Congestion tolls designed to improve the allocation of roadway space are also rent charges.

It is more difficult to set the optimal levels of such taxes compared to site value taxes, since the social costs of pollution (or congestion) are not readily measurable. This is because, insofar as air and water and roadway space (unlike farmland or building lots) are nonexclusive goods, users cannot easily be made to reveal their demand for them, though benefit-cost analysts have devised clever roundabout ways to measure benefits. Monitoring emissions often turns out to be just as problematic. Nevertheless, well-designed pollution fees or marketable permit systems are likely to improve efficiency in many cases. At least, they achieve cost-effectiveness almost automatically, if they can be enforced. This is a compelling argument for using environmental charges as a source of government revenue, in preference to the usual taxes on production and exchange. Add to it the normative judgment that the public has the *right* to collect such rents, and it becomes a Georgist argument.

Nonexclusive, depletable resources such as the atmosphere and oceans are frequently referred to as "common property" resources. This phrase, however, is used in two distinct senses. Purely nonexclusive, free-access resources are common property in the sense of *res nullius* - correctly, "nobody's property." Common property resources in the sense of *res communis* are those to which access is regulated by public controls. (Randall, 1993: 146)

The growing scarcity of environmental resources has prompted a recent trend toward public oversight and regulation of formerly unowned resources. Pollution legislation is one reflection of this trend. Another is the pressure to end the systematic underpricing of our national forests, grazing lands, water supplies, and other government-owned resources.

Georgists emphasize that even immobile land is characterized by nonexclusion in an important sense. The quality of any individual site depends on activities that take place in neighbouring regions. Land uses are scarcely less interdependent than are the uses of a certain volume of ocean or air—and not merely because pollutants migrate in the wind, rain, and ground water. Externalities abound. Ideally, perhaps, everyone would pay for the specific external costs he created, and would be compensated for the external benefit he bestowed on others. (Vickrey, 1970) But this may not be possible for nonexclusive spatial externalities. Under LVT, however, each individual, in effect, pays society for the use of positive externalities, insofar as they are accessible only from particular lands which are scarce. Symmetrically, the landowner is compensated for negative externalities by a reduction in his assessment. As Henry George expressed it:

> The tax upon land values falls upon those who receive from society a peculiar and valuable benefit, and upon them in proportion to the benefit they receive. It is the taking by the community, for the use of the community, of the value that is the creation of the community. It is the application of the common property to common uses. (George, 1879: 421)

4

The Theory of Government

Revenue Potential of the Single Tax

An important reason for the neglect of land value taxation in recent times has been the view that land rent is a small and declining proportion of national income. "Suffice it to point out," says Heilbroner (1986: 190), "that rental income in the United States has shrunk from 6 percent of the national income in 1929 to less than 2 percent today." The conclusion is drawn that LVT would not raise much revenue, and could not significantly affect the overall efficiency of the economy. Textbooks concur. Georgists have disputed this view, arguing that land rent in the United States is potentially far greater than is commonly believed. Measurements usually employed wildly underestimate the amount of privately collected land rent (after taxes) today. "Rent" as tabulated in national income accounts bears little relation to the economic rent of land. Some rent is counted as business profits and capital gains. Imputed rents are not counted at all. Statistics also fail to compensate for various methods of under-reporting taxable net rental income, including systematic underassessment of land relative to buildings by local governments. (Gaffney, 1970: 159) Some forms of rent are simply ignored; these include the rental value of rights to emit pollutants, water rights, rights of way, air and shipping routes, utility monopolies, and others. Taking these and other errors into account, Mason Gaffney concludes "that land value today is at least half of real estate, and probably more." (181)

Moreover, current actual land rent is arguably far less than it would become under the Georgist system. For one thing, building (and other) taxes are largely shifted backward to land. Exempting improvements from taxation would thus cause rents to rise. Second, since building taxes impose substantial excess burden, their removal would cause rents to rise even more than the amount of the tax "unshifting." Third, since urban renewal generates spillover benefits, to exempt buildings from taxation would put in motion agglomeration economies that further augment land rent over time.

Recall, too, that as Gaffney has shown, land taxes reallocate land from the credit-strong to the credit-weak, loosening the hold of speculators and putting land into the hands of more productive users, who impute it a higher rent.

User charges on congested public facilities (bridges, highways, parks) constitute rent, but are not counted as such. If user charges are absent, congestion may dissipate potential rent. If optimal user charges were employed and their revenue counted in rent, measured rent would rise markedly. (User charges should also include rent charges for natural resource use; e.g., water and sewer fees.)

In short, switching from the current property tax to a land value tax "lets a community socialize as much of its taxable surplus as is possible under any system of taxation." (Gaffney, 1970: 206)

Turning to the other side of the budget, Georgists also anticipate that their proposal would significantly reduce the expenses of government. The machinery of tax collection will be simplified, and bureaucratic incentives will be better aligned with the public interest. Locally, present policies generate urban sprawl at the expense of the central city, multiplying the costs of public services and "the need for a tax base." (Gaffney, 1970: 202-203) A more compact and rational pattern of land use would slash the costs of providing municipal services. Nationally, by raising real incomes and employment, tax reform would reduce social insurance programs and even expenditures for crime control. Internationally, if the Georgist philosophy were ultimately accepted worldwide, it would offer a principle for peaceful resolution of territorial conflicts, reducing military requirements.

Government as Landlord

Public sector economist Randall Holcombe defines "government" as "an organization that has the ability to finance its activities by compulsory contributions from individuals in a given geographic area." (Holcombe, 1987: 96) A government is a club whose rules apply within a geographically bounded region. An improvement district in which neighbouring landowners collectively finance a local public good, such as irrigation, is a government under this definition; so is a condominium association. A bridge club is not.

Gaffney characterizes local government as a cartel of landowners who cooperate "to supply their parcels with certain kinds of collective improvements." (Gaffney, 1962: 132) It is entirely reasonable that the "compulsory contributions from individuals in a given geographic area" be land rent charges. Indeed, the Henry George Theorem and its relatives suggest that to achieve efficient provision of public services, governments must collect land rent, supplemented where appropriate by marginal-cost user charges. (Dwyer, 1981: 55; Hotelling, 1938)

User Charges

Not only are some ordinary user charges really rent taxes, but also, all rent taxation amounts to user charges for land. Georgists advocate a dramatic reorientation of public finance: the substitution of user charges, pre-eminently land and natural resource rents, for compulsory taxes on economic activity. Rent, they say, constitutes a natural and ready fund for the support of government. It is argued that when nonproduced resources are treated as community property, and rent is taxed in preference to earned incomes, it will be easier to respect private property in produced wealth. At present, most governments perversely tax productive enterprise while leaving resource rents in private hands.

Government investment in schools, roads, parks, police, fire protection, and myriad other services intensifies the demand for land, increasing rents. It is not only efficient but also fair that these rents should be used to finance the public services which create them, rather than be forfeited to well-situated private landowners.

Rent Seeking

Gaffney observes that unproductive "rent-seeking" is likely to arise wherever surpluses are available to be shared. The surpluses resulting from urban synergy are typically shared by such inefficient means as rent controls, cross-subsidies in the pricing of government services, and in special-interest maneuvering for preferences in zoning and public expenditure. (Gaffney, 1989) LVT, by contrast, redistributes surpluses directly, fairly and efficiently. The higher is the tax rate, the smaller are the windfalls for which speculators and developers compete. Moreover, heavy reliance on LVT creates the incentive for budget-maximizing bureaucrats to adopt efficient land-use policies, since optimal policies maximize land values over all parcels. (Dwyer, 1981: 236)

Territorial Claims

Tideman argues that the Georgist principle of common property in land provides the key to solving territorial disputes worldwide. Customary justifications of territorial claims, he observes, "rest on an inconsistent combination of might-makes-right and appeal to history." (Tideman, nda: 1) He suggests that

> ....claims ought to be justified instead by a correspondence between the fraction of the world's population making a claim and the fraction of the world's territorial resources (in terms of rental value) being claimed. (Tideman, nda: 1)

If a nation's territorial claim were excessive by this standard, it could reduce the size of its claim, strive to attract immigrants, or pay compensation to those who claim less than their rightful share. (8) On this view, free competition among nations for land and citizens would result in a Tiebout world in which allocations of world resources and populations would tend to be efficient.

Common Property

Georgists view government as the guardian of the natural and social resources which are the common property of all. The single tax decreases individual and social risk, since unanticipated gains and losses utterly outside of individual landlords' control are transferred to the government and pooled with those of the whole community. Georgists argue that since land is infinitely durable, intergenerational resource misallocation occurs under a system of fee simple land tenure. A tax on rent, with assessments frequently adjusted, allows equitable distribution of resource rents, yet ensures that their services are available to the highest-valued uses.

5

The Georgist Paradigm

The Research Programme

The agenda for Georgist economic research today ranges over diverse fields. Some of the most interesting questions have been largely ignored, both by critics and by Georgists themselves. A fundamental one is the issue of whether annual rent or capitalized value is the preferred tax base. Opinions differ. George was the first to speak of land value taxation rather than rent taxation, but he appears to treat them interchangeably, never specifying the mathematical relationship between the two. Rent taxation and LVT are equivalent when rents and interest rates are stable over time, but not otherwise.

In macroeconomic theory, nonproduced land should be incorporated into models with labor, produced inputs, time, money, credit, and taxes. The role of land speculation in the business cycle, which depends on financial institutions and on expectations formation, is not yet well understood. Nor is the relationship between land tenure arrangements and long run economic growth.

In the field of public choice, Georgists can contribute to the growing literature on the incentives faced by voters, legislators, politicians, and government bureaucrats under alternative constitutional structures. There are intricate questions concerning the appropriate distribution of land rents among the different levels of a federal system. (Tideman, ndb)

Another neglected issue is the definition of the unit of assessment employed for tax purposes. Whether the assessment unit should be defined by the extent of ownership or on some other basis may have important implications for the measurement of rent and, possibly, for productive

154

incentives. (Vickrey: 1970) The problem of the assessment unit is intimately connected with a set of questions pertaining to the treatment of externalities in the Georgist program.

The Synthesis
Equity and Efficiency. It has long been standard in mainstream economics to lament a painful "trade-off" between equity and efficiency. Redistributive policies such as progressive income taxes and public assistance typically dampen productive incentives, but policies to promote economic efficiency, such as favourable tax treatment of savings or capital gains, tend to widen inequality.

According to Henry George, however, a correct interpretation of economic principles reveals that the goals of efficiency and equity are fundamentally harmonious. In particular, land rent constitutes a natural source of government revenue; its use for that purpose is both efficient and fair. More broadly, a society without economic (as well as political) justice is plagued by systemic inefficiencies, rooted in ill-managed conflict. In the very long run, growing inequality arising from institutional maladjustments can, and does, bring civilizations down. Equity is necessary for intergenerational efficiency.

Capitalism and Socialism. George wrote that both the "capitalist" ideal of individual liberty and private property and the "socialist" vision of equality and community require the public collection of resource rents for public uses. Once it is accepted that natural resources rightfully belong to everyone, there is a clear rationale for a fiscal structure which guarantees every citizen a minimum income that represents, not public charity, but the individual's rightful share of common property. At the same time, the reward of individual productive effort would be undisturbed by burdensome taxation.

In the aftermath of stunning political changes worldwide, socialism is widely perceived to have failed. Yet the Great Society has been no stunning success either. Schumpeter's confidence in the power of capitalism to eliminate poverty and want is an embarrassment today. (1950; see Sievers, 1962: 40-45) The measures of welfare capitalism, which treat the symptoms of maladjustment by forcible redistribution, hinder the efficient operation of the capitalist engine, just as Schumpeter warned—but they do not work anyway.

What Georgists propose amounts to nothing less than a new paradigm of social organization. (Harrison, 1992) They view government as the guardian of the natural and social resources which are the common property of all. Their program, by addressing the distributional failures which made socialism appear attractive or inevitable, offers an alternative which can preserve and enhance the vitality of the market system. George himself said it best:

> This revenue arising from the common property could be applied to the common benefit, as were the revenues of Sparta.... Government would change its character, and would become the administration of a great co-operative society. It would become merely the agency by which the common property was administered for the common benefit. (George, 1879: 456-457)

Increasingly, it appears, some highly regarded mainstream economists have expressed sympathy with the Georgist paradigm. A dozen years ago, for example, Kenneth Boulding wrote:

> One cannot help feeling that if only George rather than Marx had been the dominant influence on reformers in the last hundred years, again how much richer and happier the world would be. ... The neo-Georgist view ... would represent almost the only genuinely valid criticism of revolutionary Marxism in terms of Marxism's own ideals of human welfare and the abolition of poverty. (Boulding, 1982: 8-10)

Gaffney puts the case succinctly:

> Georgist policy has been shown as a means to revive dying cities, and in the process to reconcile equity and efficiency, to reconcile supply side economics with taxation, and to reconcile capital formation with taxation of the rich. It can be seen as a means of harmonizing collectivism and individualism, in the most constructive possible ways. (Gaffney, 1989: 15)

In 1990, thirty distinguished economists, Nobel prize winners among them, signed an open letter to Soviet President Mikhail Gorbachev urging him to resist public pressure to privatize land:

> (T)here is a danger that you will adopt features of our economies that keep us from being as prosperous as we might be. In particular, there is a danger

that you may follow us in allowing most of the rent of land to be collected privately. ... For efficiency, for adequate revenue and for justice, every user of land should be required to make an annual payment to the local government, equal to the current rental value of the land that he or she prevents others from using. (Tideman, et al., 1990, in Noyes, 1991: 225-228)

The Catalyst
Environmentalism. If the Georgist philosophy indeed stands ready to undergo a revival, it is easy to find the reasons. For one, the recent theoretical developments in urban economics and other fields have generated a new appreciation for the single tax. For another, in the United States at least, local governments are in deepening crisis. Georgist policy offers a ready tool for encouraging urban renewal while at the same time replenishing municipal budgets. Perhaps most significantly, environmental issues have come to the forefront of public attention, fueling a debate about how scarce natural resources, including so-called "environmental" resources, may be shared fairly and efficiently. The Georgist paradigm can potentially offer a conceptual framework and an ethical basis for integrating these and other issues of public policy.

The eleven contributors to a recent volume, *Now the Synthesis: Capitalism, Socialism, and the New Social Contract*, agree that "the world is at the crossroads of a new epoch." (Noyes, 1991: 1) It is their thesis that the philosophy of Henry George, particularly his mechanism for socializing land rent, offers a workable synthesis of capitalism and socialism which avoids the fatal flaws of each. Moreover, they suspect that the global environmental crisis will provide the catalyst for the transformation. The same conviction is expressed in another recent collection, *Commons Without Tragedy: The Social Ecology of Land Tenure* (Andelson, 1991).

Natural resource scarcity and pollution impress upon all the realization that economic land is scarce and valuable. International negotiations to manage the global commons must solve the problem of efficient allocation of yet-unowned resources and equitable distribution of their rents.

Are We All Georgists Now? Anyone familiar with the writings of Henry George can see ideas reminiscent of George cropping up in public discussions.

Supply-siders decry burdensome taxes on productive activity. Environmentalists interested in "sustainable development" seek to ensure that natural resources are shared equitably among all generations. Economists recommend effluent charges and marketable permit systems to ration the use of atmosphere and water. There are calls to increase grazing and other fees for commercial use of public lands. Development economists are beginning to admit that the problems of population and world poverty cannot be solved without radical reform of land tenure systems.

However, the presumed efficiency/equity trade-off manifests itself as a conflict between economics and environment, and few participants see how the single tax principle offers a resolution. They recognize no link between their own views and those of the forgotten "crackpot", Henry George.

The environmental crisis can be the catalyst for public acceptance of rent taxation, but both scholars and political activists must show that the sort of arguments now gaining attention for effluent fees (and the like) for the use of air and water resources apply as well to user charges for ordinary ground rent. It is necessary to explicate the connection between the Georgist rent tax, and Pigouvian taxes and subsidies designed to "internalize" externalities. (Vickrey, 1970) The treatment of depletable resources is also tied to these issues.

More broadly, whether George re-enters history in the coming years may hinge in large part on the demonstration that the Georgist paradigm not only fits with sound micro- and macroeconomic theory, but can help to unify and simplify the fields of land economics, natural resource economics, environmental economics, urban economics, and the economics of the public sector.

References

JOURNAL ABBREVIATIONS

AER	American Economic Review
AJES	American Journal of Economics and Sociology
Emtr	Econometrica
JPE	Journal of Political Economy
NRJ	Natural Resources Journal
NTA(Proc)	Proceedings of the National Tax Association
PRSA	Papers of the Regional Science Association
QJE	Quarterly Journal of Economics

Andelson, Robert V., ed. (1979), *Critics of Henry George*. London: Associated University Press.

Andelson, Robert V., ed. (1991), *Commons Without Tragedy: The Social Ecology of Land Tenure*. Savage, Maryland: Barnes and Noble.

Arnott, Richard J., and Stiglitz, Joseph E. (1979), "Aggregate Land Rents, Expenditure on Public Goods, and Optimal City Size." *QJE* 43(4): 471-500.

Boulding, Kenneth E. (1982), "A Second Look at *Progress and Poverty*." In Lindholm and Lynn, 1982: 5-18.

Brown, Harry Gunnison (1924), "The Single Tax Complex of Some Contemporary Economists." *JPE* 32: 164-190.

Brown, Harry Gunnison (1927), "Land Speculation and Land Value Taxation." *JPE* 35: 390-402.

Brown, Harry Gunnison (1928), "Taxing Rental Versus Salable Value of Land." *JPE* 36: 164-168.

Bruchey, Stuart (1972), "The Twice 'Forgotten' Man: Henry George." *AJES* 31(2): 113-138; reprinted in Lissner, 1991: 104-129.

Calvo, Guillermo A., *et. al.* (1979) "The Incidence of a Tax on Pure Rent: A New (?) Reason for an Old Answer." *JPE* 87(4): 869-874.

Cord, Steven B. (1965), *Henry George, Dreamer or Realist?* Philadelphia: University of Pennsylvania Press.

Cord, Steven B. (1985), "How Much Revenue Would a Full Land Value Tax Yield?" *AJES* 44(3): 279-293.

Davenport, H. J. (1910), "The Single Tax in the English Budget." *QJE* 24(1): 279-292.

Davenport, H. J. (1917), "Theoretical Issues in the Single Tax." *AER* 7(1): 1-30.

Dwyer, Terence Michael (1981), "A History of the Theory of Land Value Taxation." Ph.D. dissertation, Harvard University.

Dwyer, Terence Michael (1982), "Henry George's Thought in Relation to Modern Economics." *AJES* 41(4): 363-373.

Edwards, Mary Elizabeth (1988), "The Economic Effects of Taxing Land Values." Ph.D. dissertation, Texas A&M University.

Feldstein, Martin S. (1977), "The Surprising Incidence of a Tax on Pure Rent: A New Answer to an Old Question." *JPE* 85: 349-360.

Gaffney, Mason (1961), "The Unwieldy Time-Dimension of Space." *AJES* 20(5): 465-481.

Gaffney, Mason (1962), "Land and Rent in Welfare Economics." In Ackerman, Joseph, *et. al.*, eds., *Land Economics Research*. Baltimore: Johns Hopkins Press.

Gaffney, Mason (1964), "Property Taxes and the Frequency of Urban Renewal." *NTA(Proc)* 57: 272-285.

Gaffney, Mason (1964-65), "Soil Depletion and Land Rent." *NRJ* 4: 537-557.

Gaffney, Mason, ed. (1967), *Extractive Resources and Taxation*. Madison: University of Wisconsin Press.

Gaffney, Mason (1969), "Land Rent, Taxation, and Public Policy." *PRSA* 23: 141-153.

Gaffney, Mason (1970), "Adequacy of Land as a Tax Base." In Holland, 1970.

Gaffney, Mason (1973). "Tax Reform to Release Land". In Marion Clawson (ed.), *Modernizing Urban Land Policy*. Baltimore: John Hopkins Press.

Gaffney, Mason (1989), "The Role of Ground Rent in Urban Decay and Revival." *Distinguished Papers* N 89F-1, Nov. 1989. *The Henry George Lecture*, Oct. 1988. Jamaica, NY: Business Research Institute, St. John's University.

Geiger, George R. (1941), "The Forgotten Man: Henry George." *The Antioch Review* 1:3 (Sept. 1941). Reprinted in Lissner, 1991: 87-103.

George, Henry (1879), *Progress and Poverty*. New York: Robert Schalkenbach Foundation, 1971.

Harrison, Fred (1983), *The Power in the Land: An Inquiry into Unemployment, the Profits Crisis and Land Speculation*. London: Shepheard-Walwyn Publishers.

Harrison, Fred (1992), "Man and Society in the 21st Century: The Georgist Paradigm." Presented at a seminar of the American Instutite for Economic Research, Great Barrington, Mass., August 21.

Harriss, C. Lowell, ed. (1983), *The Property Tax and Local Finance*. N.Y.: Robert Schalkenbach Foundation.

Heilbroner, Robert L. (1986), *The Worldly Philosophers: The Lives, Times, and Ideas of the Great Economic Thinkers*, 3e. New York: Simon & Schuster.

Holcombe, Randall G. (1987), *Public Sector Economics*. Belmont, CA: Wadsworth.

Holland, Daniel, ed. (1970), *The Assessment of Land Value*. Milwaukee: University of Wisconsin Press.

Hotelling, Harold (1938), "The General Welfare in Relation to Problems of Taxation and of Railway and Utility Rates." *Emtr* 6: 242-269.

King, Willford I. (1924), "The Single Tax Complex Analyzed." *JPE* 32: 604-612.

Lindholm, Richard W., and Lynn, Arthur D., Jr., eds. (1982), *Land Value Taxation: The "Progress and Poverty" Centenary*. Madison: University of Wisconsin Press.

Lissner, Will, and Lissner, Dorothy, eds. (1991), *George and the Scholars*. New York: Robert Schalkenbach Foundation.

Nichols, Donald A. (1970), "Land and Economic Growth." *AER* 40(Jun): 332-340.

Noyes, Richard, ed. (1991), *Now the Synthesis: Capitalism, Socialism, and the New Social Contract*. New York: Holmes & Meier.

Randall, Alan (1993), "The Problem of Market Failure." *Natural Resources Journal* 23: 131-148. Reprinted in Dorfman, Robert, and Nancy S. Dorfman, eds., *Economics of the Environment: Selected Readings*, 3e., New York: Norton, 1993: 144-161.

Ricardo, David (1817), *The Principles of Political Economy and Taxation*. New York: E.P. Dutton and Co., 1911.

Rima, Ingrid Hahne (1986), *Development of Economic Analysis*, 4th ed. Homewood, IL: Irwin.

Rybeck, Walter (1983), "The Property Tax as a Super User Charge." In Harriss, 1983: 133-147.

Schumpeter, Joseph (1950), *Capitalism, Socialism, and Democracy*, 3rd ed. New York: Harper and Row. (First edition 1942.)

Schumpeter, Joseph (1954), *History of Economic Analysis*. New York: Oxford University Press, 1986.

Sievers, Allen M. (1962), *Revolution, Evolution, and the Economic Order*. Englewood Cliffs, N.J.: Prentice-Hall.

Skouras, Athanassios (1977), *Land and Its Taxation in Recent Economic Theory*. Athens, Greece: Papazissis.

Skouras, Athanassios (1980), "Land and Its Taxation as Issues in Economic Theory: What is the Reason for Their Eclipse?" *AJES* 39(4): 373-382.

Stiglitz, Joseph E. (1974), "The Theory of Local Public Goods." In Feldstein, Martin S., and Inman, R., eds., *The Economics of Public Services*. London: Macmillan.

Tideman, T. Nicolaus (nda) "Lasting Peace and the Justification of Territorial Claims: A Neo-Lockean Perspective." Presented at Henry George Sesquicentennial International Conference, 29 July-6 August, 1989, Philadelphia, PA.

Tideman, T. Nicolaus (ndb) "Revenue Sharing Under Land Value Taxation." Unpublished.

Tideman, Nicolaus (1990), "Open Letter to Mikhail Gorbachev." In Noyes, 1991: 225-230. With William Baumol, Robert Dorfman, Mason Gaffney, Franco Modigliani, Richard Musgrave, Robert Solow, James Tobin, William Vickrey, etc.

Yandle, Bruce, and Barnett, Andy H. (1974), "Henry George, Property Rights and Environmental Quality: Classical Answers to `New' Problems." *AJES* 33(4): 393-400.

About the Authors

KRIS FEDER, Ph.D

Dr. Feder taught economics at several Pennsylvania universities before receiving her doctorate from Temple University. She was appointed assistant professor at Bard College, Annandale-on-Hudson, New York, in 1991. She specializes in public finance and the history of economic thought. An earlier version of her paper in this book was presented to the annual meeting of the History of Economics Society, Babson College, June 12th 1994.

FRED HARRISON, M.Sc

Graduate of Oxford and London universities. Author, *The Power in the Land* (1983). He is Director of the Centre for Incentive Taxation, and Editor of the bi-monthly journal *Land & Liberty*. He is currently advising Russian municipal governments and federal government agencies on property and taxation reforms.

MICHAEL HUDSON, Ph.D

Visiting Scholar, Institute of Fine Arts, New York University. Author: *Trade, Development and Foreign Debt* (1992), and *Bronze Age Finance, 2400-900 BC* (forthcoming). Dr. Hudson has been economic adviser to US, Canadian and Mexican government agencies and to the UN Institute for Training and Research. An earlier draft of the study by Dr. Hudson in this volume was presented as a paper to the Society for Economic Anthropology (SEA) in March 1994 at Notre Dame, Indiana. It will be printed in the SEA volume on *Property: The Economic Context* (1995).

GEORGE MILLER, MD

Dr Miller, a Fellow of the Royal College of Physicians, is a senior clinical scientist with the Medical Research Council's Epidemiology and Medical Care Unit in London. He is an international expert in diseases of the heart. He was Professor in Residence in Epidemiology and Preventive Medicine at Albert Einstein College of Medicine, New York, in the 1980s.

Index